Transitioning to Online Learning During COVID-19:

Reflections by Practitioners

Angus Hooke and Greg Whateley

Table of Contents

Foreword   v

Preface   vii

SECTION 1

Chapter 1   3

The Digital Convicts of COVID-19

Greg Whateley, Emeritus Professor, GCA

Chapter 2   7

Higher Education in the 4th Industrial Age

Andrew West, Dean, UBSS

Chapter 3   13

Support for Online Teaching and Learning during
COVID-19: An Administrator's Reflections

Richard Xi, Assistant Professor, UBSS

Chapter 4   17

Transitioning from the Classroom to the Techroom

Jotsana Roopram, Assistant Professor, UBSS

Ashok Chanda, Associate Professor and Provost, UBSS Online

Greg Whateley, Emeritus Professor, GCA

Chapter 5   25

Lessons from the Transition to Online Learning:
Information Technology

Jason Whitfield, Information Technology Manager, UBSS

Chapter 6   31

Transitioning to Online Learning: More Lessons for
Information Technology

Jason Whitfield, Information Technology Manager, UBSS

SECTION 2

Chapter 7   39

Online Teaching: A Tale of Two Institutions

*Anurag Kanwar, Compliance and Continuous Improvement
Director, UBSS*

Chapter 8   43

Covid-Driven Transition to Online Teaching- a
Reflection

Syed Uddin, Assistant Professor, UBSS

Chapter 9   49

Never Lose the Moment

Art Phillips, Adjunct Professor, UBSS

Chapter 10   55

New Virtual Reality in Knowledge Transfer

Nilima Paul, Assistant Professor, UBSS

Chapter 11   59

Some Effects of COVID-19 on the Higher Education
Sector

Igor Bosma, Assistant Professor, UBSS

Chapter 12   67

Academic Integrity in an Online World: A COVID-19
Perspective

Wayne Smithson, Associate Professor, UBSS

Chapter 13   73

Online Proctoring: The Likely Future of Assessment

Jotsana Roopram, Assistant Professor, UBSS

Chapter 14   79

Reducing Students' Technostress in Online Classes:
Three Technical Methods

Arash Najmaei, Independent Marketing Consultant

Zahra Sadeghinejad, Assistant Professor, UBSS

Chapter 15   85

Reducing Students' Technostress in Online Classes:
Three Pedagogical Methods

Zahra Sadeghinejad, Assistant Professor, UBSS

Arash Najmaei, Independent Marketing Consultant

Chapter 16   91

Why the Student Voice Matters

Jotsana Roopram, Assistant Professor, UBSS

Chapter 17   95

Plugged in But Disconnected: Challenges in the 2020
Online Transition

Harry Tse, Assistant Professor, UBSS

Chapter 18   101

Work-Integrated Learning in Australian Higher
Education: An (R)Evolutionary Paradigm Shift

Wayne Smithson, Associate Professor, UBSS

Chapter 19 107

The Move to Online Learning During COVID-19:
Change, Acceptance and a Stronger You

Natasha Jacques, Assistant Professor, UBSS

Compilation of References 113

About the contributors 129

Foreword

In 859 CE, Fatima Al-Fihri established the world's first university, the University of Al-Qarawiynn (now the University of Al Quaraouiyine) in what is now Morocco. It taught Islamic studies, grammar, mathematics, and medicine, and was the first institution to confer awards for different levels of study. The delivery method comprised students sitting in a semicircle around a scholar who prompted them to read sections of text, asked them questions about the text, and explained difficult points to them. Methods of delivery in higher education have changed considerably since then. However, the pace of change has generally been imperceptible, with new practices being implemented over decades and sometimes over centuries.

The magnitude of the changes required to cope with the restrictions placed on face-to-face delivery and learning by the COVID-19 pandemic, and the pace at which these changes needed to be implemented, therefore came as a huge shock to students, lecturers, managers, and regulators in the education sector. In NSW, the Premier (Gladys Berejiklian) asked, on Tuesday 24th March 2020, that students switch immediately from onsite to home learning. In the higher education sector, the first trimester was already underway. However, within two weeks, virtually all providers including many that were only familiar with face-to-face delivery were teaching online. For most, the experience in the first few months was traumatic. But, by early 2021, enough challenges had been met, difficulties had been overcome, and unexpected benefits of online education had been impounded, to suggest that the move to online learning would not be just a temporary, stop-gap response to the pandemic, but would become the new norm.

Universal Business School Sydney (UBSS), a leading provider of business-oriented higher education in NSW, was one of the institutions required to transition to online delivery. However, it adapted relatively quickly and very successfully to the change in circumstances. This was due partly to a decision taken about a year earlier by its management to develop and commence implementing a plan for online learning. It was also due to the courage and enthusiasm shown by its students and staff to overcome the challenges and exploit the benefits of the new (to them) form of delivery.

This book contains the stories of the lecturers, technology specialists and management who guided UBSS through the challenging and tiring, but sometimes also exhilarating transition period. The experience they have acquired and the lessons they have learned provide a platform for UBSS to move confidently into the next phase of education delivery. However, these lessons and suggestions can also help other higher education providers consolidate and enhance their move into and consolidation of online learning. The chapters in this book contain easily readable and valuable information for anyone working in education or just interested in online learning.

Alan Manly OAM
Group Colleges Australia

Preface

The COVID-19 pandemic has had a huge impact on business in virtually all countries and states and in all industries. On 11th March 2020, the World Health Organisation (WHO) officially declared a COVID-19 a pandemic, the first since the "Hong Kong Flu" in 1968. More than 160 countries closed all levels of their educational facilities to contain the spread of the virus. In New South Wales (NSW), Australia, the Premier (Gladys Berejiklian) asked that students cease onsite attendance and, instead, study from home. Her request led all the state's higher education institutions to move immediately to online learning.

Some institutions in NSW had been delivering online courses for several years and had hands-on experience to help them make the transition. Others had never delivered online courses, and were moving into what, for them, was completely unchartered territory. Universal Business School Sydney (UBSS) was in the latter category but possessed one important advantage: About a year earlier, its Management had started drawing up a plan to introduce online learning, and it had a mindset and basic information that enabled it to treat the transition as being as much an opportunity as it was a challenge. This mindset did not, however, apply to most of the UBSS staff, nor to its students. This book outlines the actual experiences of managers, administrators, technology specialists and lecturers at UBSS as they worked through the transition period.

SECTION 1: THE TRANSITION FROM THE PERSPECTIVE OF MANAGEMENT

Chapter 1 looks at the experience of "digital convicts" - mainly older academics who had not expected to be engaged in, and were not prepared for, online delivery. However, UBSS went to considerable lengths to ease the transition for them. Its efforts included minimising changes and making technical support easily available by requiring lecturers to deliver their lessons on campus, refitting classrooms to be broadcasting studios and providing an intensive week-long training program on how to use digital tools and deliver classes remotely. The outcomes were generally positive, with staff becoming proficient and comfortable with online delivery, student performance being maintained, and most students (but especially postgraduate students) showing an increasing preference for online learning.

Chapter 2 foresees a growing role for online education and identifies three areas that managers of higher education institutions must pay attention to as they develop their online capabilities. First, they must focus on optimising the student learning experience. Future cohorts of students will be digital natives, and they will expect providers to make full use of the learning potential of prevailing technologies. Second, they must integrate management systems across the student learning journey. The systems must address the needs of prospective students (CRM system), current students (student, contact and learning management systems) and former students (alumni and industry partnership management systems). Third, managers must ensure that staff possess the skills and capabilities needed to keep abreast of and embrace cultural change. This includes staff learning how to modify their roles and behaviour as existing technologies are enhanced and new technologies emerge.

Responsibility for ensuring student engagement is the responsibility, not only of lecturers, but also of administrators. *Chapter 3* discusses how the administration staff at UBSS recognised and met this responsibility. They complemented the efforts of management and lecturers to maintain student engagement by ensuring that appropriate online equipment and support mechanisms were in place, proactive and friendly communications with students were maintained, and students were made fully aware of the range of resources available from the School. They also advised students of the complementary resources they would need to provide themselves in order to maximise the benefits they derived from the new mode of learning. Led by staff who had, themselves, been international students, they made a special effort to encourage students from collective cultures to adopt the more 'individualistic' and learner-centred mentality required for effective online learning.

Chapter 4 explores approaches by higher education institutions (HEIs) to implement technology-enhanced learning (TEL) and the impact of these technologies on student satisfaction, engagement, and performance. TEL embodies a basic learning management system (LMS) and various course delivery technologies. Its effectiveness can be measured in terms of enhancing the quality of learning and teaching, meeting student expectations, and improving access to learning for off-campus students. The authors suggest that an institution's successful transition to online learning requires strong leadership, implementation of appropriate online policies, adequate financial resources, integration of online technologies with digitised content, provision of technical and emotional support to students and a focus on student engagement.

Effective and enjoyable online learning requires quality technical infrastructure and readily available technical support. *Chapter 5* describes how UBSS met these requirements and discusses three lessons its IT manager learned during the transition. The first lesson was, "Don't change too much too quickly." With the IT knowledge and skills of academics and students ranging from minimal to excellent, it was important to introduce the new technology at a pace appropriate for all users. The second lesson was, "Identify correctly your customers (they are not always who you think they are!)". Initially, the IT manager believed his customers were primarily the UBSS students. Later, he added lecturers to the list. The third lesson was "Seek continuous improvement – you cannot improve what you cannot measure". Obtaining feedback from lecturers and students provides useful information on what is working and what needs to be improved.

In *Chapter 6*, the IT Manager offers three more lessons acquired or reinforced during the transition period. First, "Quality online education is not cheap!" Following the move to online learning, UBSS quickly realised that adaptations to the existing digital infrastructure would not be sufficient for quality learning. The institution had to acquire new hardware such as computers with upgraded cameras and microphones, as well as a new video conferencing delivery platform. These were expensive, but it soon became clear that the benefits to the students and the School vastly exceeded the cost. Second, "Working from home is not always the best solution". The houses and apartments of lecturers contain widely different quantities and qualities of digital equipment and at-home lecturers have vastly different levels of technical support. It is much easier to maintain a reliable and high standard of delivery by allowing the academics to deliver their lectures on campus. Third, provide "Provide training, training, and more training". There is a lot to learn for both students and staff when transitioning to online delivery, it cannot all be learned in one session, and repetition is required if retention is to be complete.

SECTION 2: THE TRANSITION FROM THE PERSPECTIVE OF LECTURERS

The key component of analysis is comparison. In *Chapter 7*, the author compares experiences during the COVID-19 induced transition to online learning of two institutions: Institution 1, which offered minimal physical and training support for staff; and Institution 2, which immediately and substantially upgraded its digital infrastructure and provided staff with an intensive training program geared to online delivery. Formal feedback indicated that students in Institution 1 were extremely dissatisfied with their experience, and many requested a refund of their tuition fees, while those in Institution 2 were very satisfied, with more than 90% indicating that they would prefer to stay online in later teaching periods.

The author of *Chapter 8* discusses his direct experience in meeting personal and pedagogical challenges during the transition to online delivery. He notes that UBSS adapted successfully to online delivery within days. He attributed this to proactive leadership, earlier investment in online resources, strong technical support, and experienced staff. He discusses his personal challenges in meeting the challenge of online learning, including fear of the unknown, limited home-office capability, and the risk of catching the virus while commuting to campus and being on campus to deliver lectures. He also discusses pedagogical challenges relating to student engagement, absence of eye-contact and body language, sustaining student interest, and maintaining student performance. He points out that, after a few weeks, he was able to overcome these challenges and become increasingly comfortable with online delivery. He concludes that online learning is now a viable alternative to onsite learning.

The need for greater student engagement is developed further in *Chapter 9*. The author notes that engagement with students has always been important but suggests that it has become even more so now that students are learning online. He outlines teaching techniques that he has acquired both as a lecturer in the higher education sector and as an onstage performer in the entertainment industry. These techniques include providing rewards for participation, requiring students to showcase their presentation skills by making 15-minute presentations, and using real-world examples to illustrate concepts and relationships.

The author of *Chapter 10* discusses the advantages and disadvantages of remote learning, including online learning, and her own experience with online delivery during the pandemic. The main advantages include any-time access, self-paced learning, near-zero classroom costs, and the ability to communicate with large audiences across global boundaries. The disadvantages include exclusion of those who do not have access to the Internet, Wi-Fi, or electric power; device breakdowns; time differences between teachers and students and among students; impersonality; cyber theft; IP issues; and the inability to mingle with other students and learn from the physical environment. The author reports that her early experience with online delivery was disappointing, with low attendance, poor attention, and limited interaction. She suggests that, to increase the effectiveness of online delivery, surveys be conducted to identify bottlenecks and mechanisms be developed to increase attendance.

Chapter 11 considers the impact of the abrupt transition from face-to-face to online learning on the student learning experience, educational outcomes, teaching, and technological innovation. The author points out that the attitude of a student to different modes of delivery depends significantly on their life circumstances with, for example, a working mother likely to have a stronger preference for online courses than a possibly younger person with few responsibilities. He also makes some interesting observations about trends in Australian universities prior to the pandemic and suggests that these could offer attractive opportunities for private education providers.

The transition from onsite to offsite education has increased the opportunities for student to cheat. In *Chapter 12*, the author uses a TEQSA framework to discuss why students cheat (opportunity, working in a second language, and dissatisfaction with teaching) and ways of reducing cheating (prevention, identification, and action). He advises that his own experiences as a lecturer suggest that prevention is the best way to reduce cheating. He then considers two approaches to supporting prevention. First, assessments can focus on small chunks, unique case-based activities, and lecturer-student communication. Second, students can be made more aware of the likelihood and consequences of being caught cheating in assessments through digital and lecturer announcements.

Chapter 13 focuses on assessment, specifically online proctoring – the invigilation of offsite exams by a human invigilator online or by artificial intelligence software. The author considers, and refutes, several concerns about online proctoring such as that it is invasive and accusatory, is inequitable, and penalises students who are unfamiliar with digital technology. She also lists many advantages of online proctoring including a wider range of assessment questions, the saving of student time, the ability to generate typed rather than hand-written answers, and a lower carbon footprint. She concludes that advancements in online proctoring tools are making online assessment at least as effective and advantageous as onsite invigilation.

The transition to online education, with its reliance on sophisticated equipment and platforms, has increased technostress among students. In *Chapter 14*, the authors discuss three technical methods that can reduce technostress. First is designing units that are interactive. They support using the three-phase model of Iteration, Response and Feedback. Second is gamification. The authors note that many gaming apps are already being used, such as Classcraft and Kahoot. Third is use of multimedia content such as recorded videos, power point presentations, vlogs, and podcasts. Multimedia content can generate a psychologically relaxed atmosphere suited to the individual preferences of students.

Chapter 15 also addresses technostress. However, in this chapter, the authors discuss three teaching methods that can reduce the stress. They are support mechanisms, online inclusivity, and scheduled repetition. Online support mechanisms include after-class consultations, online communities such as WhatsApp groups, flipped classes where students learn by teaching others, and connecting with students via online platforms such as Skype, telephone, email, and Zoom meetings. Inclusive teaching involves active listening, creating an engaging learning atmosphere, emphasising the uniqueness of each student's identity, and ensuring that the students' need to belong is satisfied. The authors refer to Ebbinghaus' forgetting curve, which becomes less steep with each reminder, to demonstrate the effect of repetition on memory, and hence its contribution to reducing technostress.

Chapter 16 notes that, in today's digital world, students expect online learning to be quick, effortless, and convenient. They also expect it to consistently meet high standards of professionalism and flexibility. Tech savvy generations live with and through technology. The culture of accessing 'real time' information has prompted speedier services and higher expectations in an exceedingly competitive service-focused sector. Providing a personal, flexible, and seamless educational experience to students can give an institution the edge to not only remain relevant but also thrive in a constantly evolving and competitive industry.

In *Chapter 17*, the author notes that while universities and colleges have been celebrating their apparently successful transition to online, the abrupt shift has left many in the industry feeling disconnected. Students have been limited in their connections with each other and their teachers, and staff are feeling isolated without the daily support of their peers. Confusion around policy within the workplace across department levels, as well as high demand for IT support and training, have led to a feeling of being overwhelmed and under supported. The chapter highlights the main challenges faced by a large postgraduate introductory economics course coordinator during the transition to online and how they were addressed.

Chapter 18 notes that the COVID-19 pandemic has had a profound effect on work practices in both academia and most business sectors. The author provides an overview of the impact on the academic arena in Australia and on the environment for Work-Integrated Learning. He argues that the pandemic brought forward changes that would have occurred anyway and concludes that in the future advanced learning may be embedded in the workplace rather than the traditional classroom.

In *Chapter 19*, the author points out that while most people recognise that change is important and desirable, they have difficulty accepting it for themselves and adjusting their behaviour to it. She uses a three-part framework developed by William Bridges Associates to explain the challenges involved in change and to describe how, in response to COVID-19, the management and staff at UBSS adjusted relatively quickly from onsite to online learning in a manner that maintained both staff morale and teaching quality.

Section 1:

The Transition from the Perspective of Management

Chapter

1

The Digital Convicts of COVID-19

Greg Whateley, Group Colleges Australia

ABSTRACT

The global pandemic has delivered an unprecedented migration to online ways of working, perhaps none more so than in the tertiary education sector. The transition to online teaching and learning came without notice and in many cases without experience, desire or expertise. This chapter shares the journey of the digital convicts of UBSS who did not sign up for online learning – but nevertheless made a very good fist of it.

INTRODUCTION

There is a consensus that Prensky (2001) was correct in his view that there are digital natives and digital immigrants – and that such personas would impact on future notions of learning and subsequently on teaching. I hasten to add that there is a third category - digital convicts - and I suggest that this category relates more to teachers than students. There may even be a case to argue that 'older' teachers are the convicts while younger 'teachers' are the immigrants.

THE COVID EFFECT

Like all education providers, Universal Business School Sydney (UBSS) was abruptly faced with the need to shift from face-to-face to online teaching. UBSS operates on a trimester model, and this need arose in Week 9 of Trimester 1, 2020. With no online class capability established at the time, the teaching staff were the epitome of digital convicts – suddenly transported to an unfamiliar 'cyber-land' by government decree in a bid to safeguard the wider populace.

The risks of this sudden pivot were not unsubstantial. They included:

- Students falling behind in their studies.
- Educators falling behind on the course schedule.
- Problems occurring with technology.
- Cost imposts of new software/technology acquisition.
- Reputational damage to the school as a whole.

Then there was, of course, the elephant in the room – the uncertainty as to how COVID would spread within Australia and how long remote learning would be necessary. Inman (2020) argued that the pandemic would be long term and would have a significant impact on international students and the Australian economy.

THE UBSS APPROACH

UBSS determined that teaching would best be delivered by teachers 'broadcasting' classes from its premises, rather than being based remotely and delivering classes on general-purpose platforms like Zoom.

While doing so incurred considerable expenditure to acquire cameras, monitors, and software at short notice, it also meant that educators could have full IT/AV on-site support. Additionally, doing so minimised disruption for our educators, enabling them to continue working in familiar surroundings and to an established routine.

To facilitate this new approach, UBSS provided an intensive training program to staff on how to utilise digital tools and deliver classes remotely during a 'pivot week', at full pay. It also implemented a 'buddy' initiative, whereby teachers were paired with full-time support staff to help them navigate their way around cyber-land.

Then, off the school went to finish the trimester.

Following the initial lockdown, attempts at introducing a hybrid model, with some students returning to campus, were thwarted by coronavirus flareups in NSW and Victoria. As such, all lessons continued to be delivered remotely.

STUDENTS MORE ENGAGED

Forefront in the minds of students and educators alike was the need to maintain teaching standards. For UBSS, metrics demonstrate that the experience has – somewhat surprisingly – delivered significant benefits for all involved, and with minimal detractions:

- Student attendance at scheduled classes increased from 70% to 80%.
- The number of students sitting examinations also rose (up 3% to 84%).
- The School maintained its impressive aggregate student feedback score of 4.2 out of a possible 5, based on 1,200+ responses (above the 78% rating of all Australian non-university higher education institutions [NUHEIs] in 2019).
- Similar results were achieved on staff feedback, with Trimester 2 returning an aggregate score of 4.2 (down only

slightly from the score of 4.4 in the immediate pre-COVID trimester).

- Educators were upskilled in course delivery and remote learning, skills that can now be utilised on an ongoing basis to reach new students and to compensate current students experiencing unplanned absences.

DIGITAL CONVICTION

The COVID situation has delivered substantial lessons for the tertiary education sector. Perhaps the most important is that our teaching professionals are highly adaptable. Navigating their way through the online landscape as digital convicts has not been easy, especially as they were required to do so at very short notice. However, educators have demonstrated not only that such a shift is possible, but also that it can deliver positive learning and business outcomes. Staff at UBSS now have the skills and experience needed to expand into offshore markets as well as the domestic-students online market, which is especially crucial given the $3 billion+ hit that border closures have had on fee revenue from locally based foreign students.

And for that, the teachers deserve full marks.

REFERENCES

Inman, M (2020) Coronavirus impact on international student numbers will be felt longer than the GFC. ABC News Live Feed. May 20 - *https://www.abc.net.au/news/2020-05-20/coronavirus-impact-on-universities-research-worse-than-gfc/12264606*

Prensky, M. (2001). On the Horizon. MCB University Press, Vol. 9 No. 5, October 2001-
https://www.marcprensky.com/writing/Prensky%20-%20Digital%20Natives,%20Digital%20Immigrants%20-%20Part1.pdf

Chapter

2

Higher Education in the 4th Industrial Age

Andrew West, Universal Business School Sydney

ABSTRACT

As the 4th industrial age impacts all of society and institutions, the accelerator that is COVID has brought this change more into focus. Higher education is one such institution which will continue to go through major change. Technology, ICT infrastructure and acceptance and expectation of younger generations of a new way of interacting at higher learning will drive the transformation. This chapter sets out the three areas that higher education providers must take account of in the new age of online learning: student learning experience, integration of management systems, and staff and student cultural change.

INTRODUCTION

We are entering the fourth industrial age. The first industrial age commenced in the late 18th century with the advent of steam power and mechanical production equipment. The second industrial age from the late 19th century came with the introduction of electricity, mass production and the division of labour. The third industrial age came in the second half of the 20th century with electronics, information technology and automated production (Schwab, 2017).

The fourth industrial age is characterized by artificial intelligence, robotics, service delivery automation and machine learning, driven by big data and having major impacts across all areas of society (Qiang, 2018). This age of industrial development has built on the previous stages and is particularly reliant on the technology and infrastructure of the third age. It "can be described as the advent of cyber-physical systems involving entirely new capabilities for people and machines … the Fourth Industrial Revolution represents entirely new ways in which technology becomes embedded within societies." (Davis, 2016).

COVID-19 has been called the great accelerator (Bradley, 2020). The whole world has had to adapt to and move quickly with many long-term trends, social movements and institutional changes happening at a much quicker pace than could have been imagined before 2020. One institution that had previously been slow to change but has been greatly impacted is higher education. It is technology, ICT infrastructure and generational change of the acceptance and expectation of a new way of interaction at higher learning that will continue to drive this change in higher-educational institutions.

To enable this change and take advantage of the opportunities being presented in the 4th industrial age, higher-education providers must be cognizant of and plan across three main areas:

1. Optimizing the student learning experience.
2. Integrating management systems across the student learning journey.
3. Ensuring that staff embrace cultural change and develop skills and capabilities while embedding automation and technology within the organisation.

OPTIMIZING THE STUDENT LEARNING EXPERIENCE

There is no 'one size fits all' in the delivery of higher education. As more students enter higher education as digital natives, their expectation and acceptance of the digital interface will become more pervasive.

First and foremost is a focus on the student learning experience, which involves an understanding of the various learning styles, cultural backgrounds, motivations for learning, student's capacity for learning and level of engagement with the subject material.

INTEGRATING MANAGEMENT SYSTEMS ACROSS THE STUDENT LEARNING JOURNEY

To ensure that there is a focus on the learning experience, the student learning journey must be understood throughout the students' contact with the organisation. The relationship with the student changes throughout the student journey and must be catered for. To gain this understanding and capture data to inform decisions, management systems must be designed for the characteristics of the student/provider interaction. These systems are:

- Prospective student - customer relationship management system.
- Admissions and student performance - student management system.
- Student support - contact management system.
- Learning environment - learning management system.
- Post-graduation - alumni and industry partnership management system.

The success of the student learning journey is dependent on a seamless student interaction with the provider as they move through the various stages.

STAFF CULTURAL CHANGE

A higher education provider cannot simply focus on developing the skills and capabilities needed to design, develop, deploy, and maintain the introduction of new technologies and systems. As automation, bots and artificial intelligence are introduced, higher education providers will need to redesign worker roles, assigning some to staff, others to machines, and still others to a hybrid role in which technology augments and supports human performance.

The term 'no-collar workers' has been used to describe the range of virtual workers, cognitive agents, bots, and other AI-driven capabilities (Deloittes, 2018). There has been much written about the vocations that may be replaced during this time of change. Studies that have been replicated across the USA, UK and Australia indicate that there is a high probability that at least 40% of existing jobs will be replaced by automation during the next 10 years (CEDA, 2015). Higher education is one industry where automation will have a large impact on all types of work across all roles.

Rather than viewing the advent of the 4th Industrial Age as a threat to jobs, higher education providers must take staff with them along this journey of change. This will involve highlighting that the no-collar workers complement the collar workers, improving work practices and providing a higher level of student experience. Having a clear vision of what the future of a higher education provider will be in the 4th Industrial Age and communicating this clearly and regularly to staff will ensure that all are on board with the cultural change that is occurring.

REFERENCES

Bradley C, Hirt, M, Hudson S, Northcote N, Smit S (2020) The Great Acceleration. *https://www.mckinsey.com/business-functions/strategy-and-corporate-finance/our-insights/the-great-acceleration. Viewed 2nd April 2021.*

CEDA (2015). Australia's Future Workforce. *https://www.ceda.com.au/ResearchAndPolicies/Research/Workforce-Skills/Australia-s-future-workforce.* Viewed 30th March 2021.

Davis N (2016). What is the Fourth Industrial Revolution? *https://www.weforum.org/agenda/2016/01/what-is-the-fourth-industrial-revolution/.* Viewed 29th March 2021.

Deloittes (2018). No-collar workforce: Humans and machines in one loop— collaborating in roles and new talent models. *https://www2.deloitte.com/us/en/insights/focus/tech-trends/2018/no-collar-workforce.html.* Viewed 31st March 2021.

Qiang (2018) The Fourth Revolution, *https://en.unesco.org/courier/2018-3/fourth-revolution.* Viewed 31st March 2021.

Schwab, K (2017) The Fourth Industrial Revolution. Penguin UK, Great Britain.

Chapter

3

Support for Online Teaching and Learning During COVID-19: An Administrator's Reflections

Richard Xi, Universal Business School Sydney

ABSTRACT

One of the key challenges in safeguarding the quality of learning during the COVID-induced transition to online delivery was maintaining student engagement. Meeting this challenge was a responsibility, not only of managers and lecturers, but also of administrators. At UBSS administrative staff in all areas and at all levels promoted engagement during the transition period by ensuring that appropriate online equipment and support mechanisms were in place, by maintaining proactive and friendly communications with students, and by ensuring that students were fully aware both of the range of resources available from the School and of the complementary resources students would need to provide themselves in order to maximise the benefits they could receive from the new mode of learning.

THE CONTEXT

The COVID-19 pandemic precipitated a dramatic, virtually overnight change in the provision of higher education, away from the comfortable, centuries-old mode of on-campus and face to face (F2F) learning and teaching to off-campus and online delivery. The suddenness and scale of the transition were generally unforeseen, and few educational institutions had the resources and experience to adjust easily to them. The move presented many problems for senior management who were faced with a sharp reduction in revenues, increased demands for equipment and training, and an urgent need to adopt new strategies and introduce new procedures. It presented equally difficult challenges for academics who had to adapt quickly to unfamiliar methods of delivery and assessment. However, the pandemic also gave rise to challenges for the less visible workers, the administrators. At UBSS, a major goal for the administration staff was to provide appropriate administrative complements to the efforts of managers and lecturers to maintain student engagement.

Following the transition, students quickly became aware of the benefits of online learning, such as shorter travelling times and lower commuting costs. However, they were also faced with significant challenges, particularly those international students who had no prior experience with online learning in an overseas setting. Administrators at UBSS, who undertake most of the one-on-one communication with students, quickly became aware of the nature and scale of these challenges.

THE CHALLENGES AND APPROACHES

Carla Blakey and Claire Major, researchers at the University of Alabama, point out that 'engagement requires a psychological investment on the part of the learner as well as persistence in undertaking the learning task' (Blakey, 2015). A key objective in safeguarding the quality of learning following the COVID-induced move to online delivery was to ensure that students continued to make this psychological investment in their learning and to maintain their persistence as learners. At the administrative level, this objective was pursued through careful management by the administration staff of online learning processes and activities, including:

- Being technically ready. UBSS technical staff worked around the clock to ensure that the School's online equipment was up-to-date, internet access was reliable and expert technical staff were on hand to support the new mode of learning. The administrative staff also quickly recognised the value of longer lead times, and prior to the first full trimester of online learning, informed students well in advance of all technology-related requirements for the coming learning period. This was especially important for students who were accessing online classes from their home country.

- Ensuring that teaching and administrative staff as well as students were familiar and comfortable with the online learning methods being used, including the online course structures and content developed by the academics and the learning management system (LMS) used by the School. UBSS' smooth-functioning, web-based information hub provided an excellent platform for accommodating the need of students to share their online learning concerns and to explore with staff and each other suitable responses to them.

- Providing students with the administrative and learning support they required, such as information about online course arrangements, timetable selections, and assessment processes including the new practice (for UBSS) of online examinations.

- Helping students achieve cognitive readiness for and be proactive about online learning. Many students, especially those in the early stages of an undergraduate degree, lack an adequate appreciation of their role as commander-in-charge of their own learning and of the need to take personal responsibility for acquiring the knowledge, skills and other resources needed for enjoyable and effective learning, including online learning.

- Being aware of and responsive to the cultural aspects of online learning. Some Asian students (particularly those who had recently arrived in Australia) experienced difficulties in the early stage of the transition as they felt 'lonely' and 'isolated' in the new, off-campus environment. This was largely because they come from a cultural environment that is dominated by a 'collectivist' value system. It requires time and support to pivot their mindset toward an 'individualistic', learner-centred mentality and toward more autonomous behaviour. The administrative staff were patient but persistent in helping students make this pivot.

CONCLUSION

The experience at UBSS showed that forward-looking and positive support by administration staff across the whole institution can make an important contribution to helping students adjust to change, and to maintain a high level of engagement with the institution, lecturers, and fellow students. Most of the steps taken by administrators are small, affecting individual students in specific and often unique situations. However, cumulatively, these steps can be quite large, and can change a good result into a great outcome, both for the institution and for the students.

REFERENCES

Blakey, C & Major, C 2019, 'Student Perceptions of Engagement in Online Course: An Exploratory Study', Online Journal of Distance Learning Administration, vol. XXII, no. 4., viewed 20 March 2021, *https://www.westga.edu/~distance/ojdla/winter224/blakeymajor224.html*

Chapter

4

Transitioning from the Classroom to the Techroom

Jotsana Roopram, Universal Business School Sydney

Ashok Chanda, Universal Business School Sydney

Greg Whateley, Universal Business School Sydney

ABSTRACT

The COVID-19 pandemic forced higher education institutions (HEIs) in Australia to transition from the classroom to the techroom by adopting Technology-Enhanced Learning (TEL), in order to remain current and competitive in the sector. This chapter explores approaches by HEIs to implement TEL strategies and the impact of these approaches on student satisfaction, engagement, and performance.

INTRODUCTION

TEL embodies a basic learning management system (LMS) and various course delivery technologies. Its meaning in higher education differs from institution to institution (Laurillard, 2009; Oliver, 2005) and is defined in terms of three key factors: enhancing the quality of learning and teaching; meeting student expectations; and improving access to learning for off-campus students (James, 2010; Walker, 2012; Walker, 2014).

TEL's benefits include enhanced engagement, flexible learning, long-distance collaboration, asynchronous communication, development of time-management skills and enhanced learning outcomes (Clark, 2011; González, 2010). This inimitable delivery of education (Martinez, 2020) provides an opportunity for Australian leaders to shift the existing educational paradigm.

CHANGING PARADIGM – VANISHING CLASSROOMS AND EMERGING TECHROOMS

The pandemic significantly impacted the educational landscape. According to UNESCO (2020), governments in 161 countries closed all levels of educational facilities to contain the spread of the virus, affecting over 60% of the global student population. To mitigate this impact, many HEIs continued with or moved to online learning.

Effective online learning depends on student access to technological resources (Lamb, 2020), technological 'know-how' (Noble, 2020), appropriate technical infrastructure by the HEIs (ACER, 2020; Anderson, 2020), delivery capability by the academic staff (ACER, 2020; Lamb, 2020; Toth-Stub, 2020), reliable internet connection and, for some, dedicated online software. Yet, even in Australia, where 'access to digital technologies and the internet is high', many students have limited access to technological resources (Clinton, 2020).

TRANSITIONING OF AN INSTITUITION TO TEL

The Australasian Council on Open, Distance and e-Learning (ACODE) has developed a TEL Framework comprising eight aspects of TEL implementation: Strategy, Quality, Systems, Services, Staff Development, Staff Support, Student Training, and

Student Support. This blueprint for institutions delivering TEL encourages the adoption of all eight elements.

Leadership is key in transitioning to TEL. In addition, online policy implementation and planning, financial resources, content digitisation and its delivery, strong student support and enhancing student engagement, are all important (Bates, 2011).

Leadership support

Effective online delivery requires that leaders possess relevant skills and knowledge and a have a positive attitude (Northouse, 2013

Implementation of online policy and planning

As a critical area in transitioning to online learning (Bates, 2011), HE institutions should implement policies to support pedagogical awareness surrounding learning. Integration of online learning into HEI's policies will increase relevance for, and foster greater adoption by, stakeholders (Casanova, 2018).

Providing financial resources

The economic downturn and border closures caused by the pandemic placed significant financial pressure on HEIs (Kim, 2020) and generated a considerable enrolment deficit. Online delivery required more financial resources, creating an additional financial burden.

Content digitisation and its delivery

For effective learning, both online learning technologies and online digitised content must be integrated (Cheawjindakarn, 2012). A quality online learning experience requires high standards of instructional design, development, and analysis, as well as faculty and student support (Martin, 2017). Timely and constructive feedback between students and lecturers provides critical input for enhancing student engagement (Al-Bashir, 2016).

Building strong student support

In the absence of on-site learning, technical support should be offered (Jaggars, 2014). HEIs' key focus should remain on student health and well-being, considering the emotional distress some students faced due to the pandemic (Roy, 2020).

Enhancing student engagement

Educational technology contributes to student engagement in online learning (Krause, 2008), fosters enriched class discussions, increases student knowledge, and creates a collaborative learning environment (Kahn, 2017).

MAKING TEL A SUCCESS – LEARNER SATISFACTION, ENGAGEMENT AND PERFORMANCE

With online learning becoming essential in 2020, sharper focus was needed on student satisfaction, engagement, and performance.

Online lectures have a greater impact on student perceptions than do face-to-face lectures. Online teaching is more challenging for instructors because it requires the adoption of new techniques and strategies to produce quality learning experiences (Asoodor, 2014).

Student engagement can be identified in the development of critical thinking skills, achieving higher grades, and embracing learning to achieve intrinsically motivated goals. Gonzalez et al. (2020) analysed the effects of the pandemic confinement on student performance. Their study revealed that confinement moved student learning strategies toward a more continuous online study approach which increased learning efficiency.

Online delivery that is well-designed and conducted within a robust learning management system by skilled teachers offers a comparable learning experience to face-to-face delivery (Toth-Stub, 2020). TEL, with fully supported active online learning, can deliver high retention and attainment rates leading to a rising demand for superior quality online education (Panigrahi, 2018).

CONCLUSION

Today's students are accustomed to using digital platforms. They recognise poor digital design and disengage quickly with inadequate online experiences. Therefore, there is a demand for high quality, supported online learning, both in Australia and globally. HEIs need to embrace and leverage the changing face of education by adapting to the sector's fluctuating needs with appropriate leadership, policy planning, financial resources, and student support as well as with innovative content digitisation and delivery.

TEL has transformed into a delivery approach that encourages and embraces the potential of both technology and people for greater retention and improved performance. Online students have been 'unseen' most of the time. However, with enhanced TEL strategies in place, students can now be 'visible' using the entire-institution approach to greatly improve learning outcomes.

REFERENCES

Al-Bashir, M., Kabir, R., and Rahman, I. (2016). The value and effectiveness of feedback in improving students' learning and professionalizing teaching in higher education. Journal of Education and Practice, 7(16), 38-41.

Anderson, J. (2020). The Coronavirus Pandemic is Reshaping Education. Quartz Daily Brief. Retrieved from *https://qz.com/1826369/how-coronavirus-is-changing-education/*

Asoodar, M., Vaezi, S., and Izanloo, B. (2016). Framework to improve e-learner satisfaction and further strengthen e-learning implementation. Computers in Human Behavior, 63, 704-716.

Australian Council for Educational Research (ACER). (2020). Ministerial Briefing Paper on Evidence of the Likely Impact on Educational Outcomes of Vulnerable Children Learning at Home during COVID-19. Paper prepared for the Australian Government Department of Education, Skills and Employment.

Bates, A. W., and Sangra, A. (2011). Managing Technology in Higher Education: Strategies for transforming teaching and learning. San Francisco, CA: Jossey-Bass Higher and Adult Education Series.

Casanova, D., and Price, L. (2018). Moving towards sustainable policy and practice–a five level framework for online learning sustainability. Canadian Journal of Learning and Technology, 44(3).

Cheawjindakarn, B., Suwannatthacote, P., and Theeraroungchaisri, A. (2012). Critical success factors for online distance learning in higher education: A review of the literature. Creative Education, 8(3), 61-66.

Clark, B. (2011). Moving the technology into the AU/LBS Classroom Project: Blended delivery: A literature review. Ontario: Ministry of Training, Colleges and Universities. Retrieved from *http://www.hpedsb.on.ca/ec/elearning/documents/BeaClarkes-Blendedlearningreview.pdf*

Clinton, J. (2020). Supporting Vulnerable Children in the Face of a Pandemic. Paper prepared for the Australian Government Department of Education, Skills and Employment. Melbourne, Australia: Centre for Program Evaluation, Melbourne Graduate School of Education, The University of Melbourne.

Gonzalez T, de la Rubia MA, Hincz KP, Comas-Lopez M, Subirats L, Fort S, et al. (2020) Influence of COVID-19 confinement on students' performance in higher education. PLoS ONE 15(10).

González, C. (2010). What do university teachers think eLearning is good for in their teaching? Studies in Higher Education, 35, 61–78.

Jaggars, S. S. (2014). Choosing between online and face-to-face courses: Community college student voices. American Journal of Distance Education, 28(1), 27-38.

James, R., Krause, K.-L., and Jennings, C. (2010, October 1). The first-year experience in Australian universities: Findings from 1994–2009. Canberra: Commonwealth of Australia. Retrieved from *http://www.griffith.edu.au/__data/assets/pdf_file/0006/37491/FYERep ort05.pdf*

Kahn, P., Everington, L., Kelm, K., Reid, I., and Watkins, F. (2017). Understanding student engagement in online learning environments: The role of reflexivity. Education Technology and Research Development, 65, 203-218.

Kim, C., and Woodland, D. (2020). Navigating the Financial Impact on COVID-19 on Higher Education. Retrieved from *https://www.kaufmanhall.com/ideas-resources/article/*

Krause, K. L., and Coates, H. (2008). Students' engagement in first-year University. Assessment and Evaluation in Higher Education, 33(5), 493-505.

Lamb. S. (2020). Impact of Learning from Home on Educational Outcomes for Disadvantaged Children: Brief Assessment. Paper prepared for the Australian Government Department of Education, Skills and Employment by the Centre for International Research on Education Systems and the Mitchell Institute. Victoria University.

Laurillard, D., Oliver, M., Wasson, B., and Hoppe, U. (2009). Implementing technology enhanced learning. In N. Balacheff, S. Ludvigsen, T. de Jong, A. Lazonder, S. Barnes, and L. Montandon (Eds.), Technology-enhanced learning: Principles and products (pp. 289–306). Berlin: Springer Science+Business.

Martin, F., Polly, D., Jokiaho, A., and May, B. (2017). Global standards for enhancing quality in online learning. The Quarterly Review of Distant Education, 18(2), 1-10.

Martinez, E. (2020). Pandemic Shakes Up World's Education Systems. Retrieved from *https://www.hrw.org/news/2020/03/19/pandemic-shakes-worlds-education-systems*

Noble, K. (2020). COVID-19 School Closures Will Increase Inequality Unless Urgent Action Closes the Digital Divide. Opinion. 3 April 2020. Victoria University. Retrieved from *http://www.mitchellinstitute.org.au/opinion/covid19-digital-divide/*

Northouse, P. G. (2013). Leadership: Theory and practice (6th ed.). Thousand Oaks, CA: Sage.

Oliver, M., and Trigwell, K. (2005). Can 'blended learning' be redeemed? E-Learning, 2, 17–26.

Panigrahi, R., Srivastava, P. R. and Sharma, D. (2018). Online learning: Adoption, continuance and learning outcome – A review of literature, International Journal of Information Management, 43, 1-14.

Roy, D., Tripathy, S., Kar, S. K., Sharma, N., Verma, S. K., and Kaushal, V. (2020). Study of knowledge, attitude, anxiety and perceived mental healthcare need in Indian population during COVID-19 pandemic. Asian Journal of Psychiatry, 51, 1-8.

Toth-Stub, S. (2020). Countries Face an Online Education Learning Curve: The coronavirus pandemic has pushed education systems: Online, testing countries' abilities to provide quality learning for all - retrieved from *https://www.usnews.com/news/best-countries/articles/2020-04-02/coronavirus-pandemic-tests-countries-abilities-to-create-effective-online-education*

UNESCO (2020). Education: From disruption to recovery. Retrieved from https://en.unesco.org/news/covid-19-learning-disruption-recovery-snapshot-unescos-work-education-2020.

Walker, R., Voce, J., Ahmed, J., Nicholls, J., Swift, E., Horrigan, S., and Vincent, P. (2014). 2014 survey of technology enhanced learning: Case studies. Oxford: Universities and Colleges Information Systems Association. Retrieved from *http://www.ucisa.ac.uk/groups/dsdg/asg/~/media/7BCB3F2FF0E141 A79A66BC87DDB34A14.ashx*

Walker, R., Voce, J., and Ahmed, J. (2012). 2012 survey of technology enhanced learning for higher education in the UK. Oxford: Universities and Colleges Information Systems Association. Retrieved from *http://www.ucisa.ac.uk/groups/ssg/surveys.aspx*

Chapter

5

Lessons from the Transition to Online Learning: Information Technology

Jason Whitfield, Universal Business School Sydney

ABSTRACT

In April 2020, UBSS was forced by the COVID-19 pandemic to move from face-to-face to online lesson delivery. The Information Technology (IT) Manager at UBSS was assigned the daunting task of implementing and testing, within a very short timeframe, all the IT infrastructure that would be required. In this chapter, he discusses his expectations at the start of the transition and how they changed as the move to online learning was being implemented. He also shares three lessons he received during the transition.

LESSON 1: DO NOT CHANGE TOO MUCH, TOO QUICKLY

For most UBSS staff, the transition to online lesson delivery was the most significant change in their working life in a very long time. I know that it was the most significant change for me during my 15 years with the School.

There is always a temptation when faced with the need for sudden change, to be all "gung-ho", and change too many things too quickly (Nilson, 2017). When UBSS made the decision to introduce online learning, I immediately thought of all the new technology (both hardware and software) that we would need. I initially believed that due to the need to move quickly, we should make as many changes as we could as soon as we could.

What brought me back to reality was the realisation that I would not be the one using this new technology – it would be the lecturers and, to a lesser degree, the students. Since their IT skills ranged from excellent to minimal, and the system had to serve all users, I realised that changes had to be made in small steps. Hence, the initial transition to online learning consisted of leveraging our existing (and proven) hardware and software to get things going, and then implementing new technology one small step at a time. This incremental approach conferred two benefits: first, the lecturers did not have to learn many new procedures right at the start; and secondly, I had time to test new technologies thoroughly before implementing them.

Since this introductory phase was completed, the technology used at UBSS for online learning has been continuously improved and expanded. But it has been done slowly and very carefully.

The key lesson here: When implementing new technology, slow and steady wins the race.

LESSON 2. IDENTIFY YOUR CUSTOMERS (THEY ARE NOT ALWAYS WHO YOU THINK THEY ARE!)

When UBSS started the journey towards online learning, I firmly believed that our top priority was to take care of our customers. And at the time, I thought that our students were our customers. After all, they are the ones who purchase our product and thus support our business. However, I later realised that from an IT perspective, the "customer base" is much wider. In fact, it comprises every person who uses any part of the UBSS IT infrastructure. It therefore includes all our staff and students.

This became very clear soon after the decision was made to introduce a high-quality online learning infrastructure system. In addition to asking the question "How easy would this be for our students to use?", I had to ask, "How easy would this be for our lecturers to use?" If the lecturers have difficulty using a new technology, it will not matter if the students find it easy or not – the student experience will suffer regardless. In fact, it could be argued that the "lecturer experience" is even more critical for online learning, since how the lecturer performs when delivering an online lecture is probably the most influential part of the student online learning experience.

> **The key learning here: Anyone who interacts with the IT infrastructure must be considered a "customer".**

LESSON 3. SEEK CONTINUOUS IMPROVEMENT – AND YOU CANNOT IMPROVE WHAT YOU DO NOT MEASURE!

I have always believed in the philosophy of continuous improvement for any IT-related system. With the adoption of online learning, this conviction has become even stronger.

It may be tempting to just set up an online lesson delivery platform and wish the lecturers "good luck!". But if you want to improve the student experience, you must look for ways to enhance both the reliability and usability of the platform (Dharwan, 2019). This can be done in many ways. Some are obvious, such as asking for feedback from both lecturers and students as to what they like (and do not like) about the platform. Others, however, are more subtle.

For example, if you want your online lessons to be professional, you will want to minimize the incidence of IT equipment failures. How many times have you joined an online meeting, only to find that one or more participants cannot get their camera or microphone to work? My solution to this problem is a combination of careful system design and constant monitoring.

Careful system design involves implementing technology in such a way that it cannot be used incorrectly (such as ensuring that microphones and cameras are automatically always on) and minimising the possibility for human error (such as putting locking-out controls on equipment so it cannot be inadvertently mis-configured).

Constant monitoring is the other key part – having automated systems in place that check the equipment that the lecturers use to ensure that it is working correctly. Another benefit is that if an item of equipment does fail, corrective action can be taken immediately.

> **The key learning here: Online education depends on reliable IT infrastructure, and careful design and monitoring is the only way this can be achieved.**

CONCLUSION

Successful online education requires much more than a laptop and webcam. Given the extremely competitive nature of the education market, students do not have to, and will not, put up with content and delivery that do not mesh with quality online infrastructure, and therefore cannot generate strong student engagement.

However, if an institution takes a "big-picture" approach to the implementation of online learning and considers technology within the broader context of the customer experience, it can be a leader in this challenging new world of online education.

REFERENCES

Dhawan, S. (2019). Online Learning: A Panacea in the Time of COVID-10 Crisis. Journal of Educational Technology systems. Volume 49, Issue 1.

Nilson, L., Goodson, L. (2017). Online Teaching at its Best: Merging Instructional Design with Teaching and Learning Research. Wiley.

Chapter

6

Transitioning to Online Learning: More Lessons for Information Technology

Jason Whitfield, Universal Business School Sydney

ABSTRACT

In April 2020, UBSS moved from face-to-face to online lesson delivery. The IT Manager realised that the transition would not only be challenging but would also be a learning experience. In Chapter 5, he listed three lessons he learned from the experience: Do not change things too quickly; focus on the needs of your customers; and monitor for continuous improvement. In this chapter, he adds three more lessons: Quality online education is not cheap; lectures are better delivered from campus than the lecturer's home; and ongoing training should be provided for both staff and students.

LESSON 1: QUALITY ONLINE EDUCATION IS NOT CHEAP

Before the COVID pandemic, UBSS was very successful in its delivery of face-to-face learning. This was due partly to the large capital investments it had been made over many years to provide lecturers and students with technology that was up-to-date and supported this mode of delivery. However, when UBSS made the move to online learning, it became apparent very quickly that the existing infrastructure (both hardware and software) could not provide online education that was comparable in quality to that achieved in a face-to-face environment.

Due to the speed at which UBSS was required to make the transition to online delivery, its initial step was to adapt existing technology as best it could to the new delivery mode. The adaptations were an improvement, but Management quickly realised that much better classroom equipment and software platforms were needed if excellent student outcomes were to be achieved. Simple items such as cameras and microphones are not required for face-to-face classes but become critical for online delivery (O'Loughlin, 2020). Although the PCs at UBSS already had these features built-in, their quality and flexibility were clearly unsatisfactory. Replacing them with higher quality versions was undertaken, but at considerable cost. However, subsequent student feedback indicated that the expenditures were justified.

The software also required attention. The existing video conferencing platform could have been used for online delivery (and initially it was), but it soon became apparent that it did not possess enough of the features needed for effective student engagement. Thus, more capital was invested in a totally new software platform for online delivery. Student feedback and retention rates indicated, again, that this expenditure paid off.

> **The key issue here: An institution that attempts to deliver online learning without spending money on supporting technology will fail, and its customers will vote with their feet.**

LESSON 2: WORKING FROM HOME IS NOT ALWAYS THE BEST SOLUTION

I have heard it touted many times that a side benefit of online lesson delivery is allowing lecturers to deliver their lessons from any location including their own home. Whilst working from home is very convenient for lecturers, UBSS learned very early on that it had two profoundly negative effects. First, consistency of delivery was lost. Each lecturer had a different camera, a different microphone, different lighting and, crucially, a different internet connection. Secondly, quality was reduced. For online learning, a reliable internet connection is the most crucial component of technology, as it directly affects the student experience. Although penetration of the NBN has improved the situation in recent years, we found that several lecturers had internet connectivity that was simply not fast or reliable enough.

When variable connectivity is combined with differences in the quality of equipment being used, a student can have an excellent online experience in one class but a very poor experience in the next. Importantly, this can occur when the lecturers in both classes are well-liked and personally engaging. Even a great lecturer can easily be let down by a camera that does not show their face clearly, a microphone that does not pick up their voice accurately, and an internet connection that continually drops out.

Another issue that was revealed early on is that when lecturers deliver their lessons from home, it can be very difficult and time consuming for them to get technical support when things go wrong. The shift from face-to-face to online lesson delivery has placed far more reliance on technology, and if the latter fails, there is no fall-back position. With face-to-face delivery, the lecturer always has the option of standing in front of the class and chatting away if they cannot get their data projector or PC to work. They cannot do this when they are teaching online from their home and the internet connection fails.

Realising that all of this could adversely affect the student experience, UBSS Management decided very early on that all UBSS lecturers would deliver their online lessons from their normal UBSS classrooms. These are set up with the same high-quality equipment, ensuring a consistently high level of online delivery. Having the lecturers onsite also allows for technical support to be always available, enabling issues to be resolved quickly.

> **The key issue here: Working from home is convenient for the lecturers, but there is a price to be paid. That price is an inconsistent and often poor student experience.**

LESSON 3. PROVIDE TRAINING, TRAINING, AND MORE TRAINING

The transition to online learning during the COVID pandemic could not have been foreseen by anyone, including our lecturers. They had been happily delivering lectures to a live audience for years, when suddenly, they were told: "We're moving online. You have one week to prepare."

This was a huge shock to the lecturers, none of whom had originally "signed up" for online delivery. They were forced to adapt – and more importantly, they were forced to use technology in ways they had never used it before.

From my perspective, one of the key challenges during the transition period was ensuring that staff "at the coal face" – i.e., the lecturers – were adequately trained in the use of online technology. Not only that, but they also needed to be comfortable with the technology, so they could be relaxed during their classes and engaging with their online audience.

Thorough training is essential, and not just for the lecturers. Providing "how to" guides for students is also crucial, as well as demonstrating any new technology to the management, administration, and marketing departments. Keeping everyone "in the loop", builds confidence within the entire organisation.

As the person responsible for providing the training, I also learned that the nature of the training must match the aptitude level of each lecturer (McClure, 2018). Each lecturer has a different level of familiarity with the technology being used, and it is therefore necessary to give more time to those lecturers who appear to be uncomfortable using it.

Periodic re-training was also found to be very useful. After UBSS had been delivering lessons online for several months, I could see both what lecturers were doing right and where they could improve in their use of technology. I was able to incorporate my findings into future training sessions with the goal of improving the student experience.

> **The key issue: Training staff in the use of new technology is as important as the technology itself. Perhaps more important. After all, the technology is useless if the end users cannot take advantage of it.**

CONCLUSION

I knew that the move to online learning would not be easy, inexpensive, or quick. I was proved right on all three points. However, I was surprised at just how difficult, how expensive, and how long the transition would be.

If the goal of the educational institution is to deliver online learning in a manner that is professional and sets the institution apart from its competitors, it must be prepared to spend money, to overcome many difficult technical issues and, most importantly, to allow sufficient time for the changes to be implemented. Transitions of this nature cannot be rushed.

REFERENCES

McClure, K. (2018). Catering to individual differences. Language magazine. *https://www.languagemagazine.com/2018/06/11/catering-to-individual-differences/*

O'Loughlin, D. (2020). Selecting teaching resources that meet student needs: A guide.
https://www.acer.org/au/discover/article/selecting-teaching-resources-that-meet-student-needs-a-guide

Whitfield, J. (2008). Lessons from the Transition to Online Learning: Information Technology. UBSS Publications Series.

Section 2:

The Transition from the Perspective of Lecturers

Chapter

7

Online Teaching: A Tale of Two Institutions

Anurag Kanwar, Universal Business School Sydney

ABSTRACT

In early 2020, the COVID-19 pandemic forced education providers to move from onsite to online delivery. This article explores the author's personal experience of the transition as a casual lecturer across two higher education institutions and concludes with reflections on the changing state of education.

PRIOR TO COVID-19

That COVID-19 disrupted the provision of higher education is a given. Time will tell how history judges this disruption (Taleb, 2007), but prior to 2020 the use of educational videos, though increasing, was often cursory and was generally seen as an add-on to traditional methods rather than the main event in teaching (Dart, 2020). In fact, many experienced academics considered that YouTube and other online platforms were largely a waste of time. What students really wanted, they suggested, was a face-to-face experience.

THE IMPACT OF COVID-19

The NSW government ordered a lockdown on Wednesday 18th of March 2020. People could only leave their residence if they had a recognised justification such as carrying out essential work, buying food or coping with a medical emergency. Travelling to attend classes in a school or other educational institution was permitted only when a student could not learn from their residence. The lockdown caused many educational institutions to rush into online delivery, frantically uploading all teaching materials to an online learning platform and requiring their staff to immediately commence online delivery from their homes.

THE INSTITUTIONAL RESPONSES

Institution 1

On the Friday immediately following announcement of the lockdown, one higher education provider with whom the author had personal experience, referred to here as Institution 1, simply sent all academic staff an email stating that from the following Monday they would have to deliver all their material online. The lecturers, most of whom were casual staff, were directed to use Zoom. No additional assistance or support was provided. The Institution left it to the lecturers to decide how to adjust learning materials and assessments and to ensure that their online equipment was up to the task. The lecturers ended up forming ad hoc WhatsApp groups to aid each other.

Institution 2

The second provider, referred to as Institution 2, also took the initial step of sending an email to lecturers. However, this email advised lecturers that classes would be suspended for two weeks, to allow both staff and students to prepare for the move to online learning. Lecturers were told to come to campus to deliver lectures and were provided with purpose-designed studios that were equipped with state-of-the-art facilities and cameras. Thus, there was no pressure on lecturers to upgrade home-office equipment, which was in short supply following announcement of the lockdown.

THE RESULTS

Institution 1

This lecturer commenced by providing classes on Zoom from her home, as required by the Institution. But she was using a free account, and after 45 minutes the first class was ended when another class started. The lecturer then directed students to Google Hangouts where they completed the session. The lecturer provided feedback to management about the platform issue. No solution was offered, and the lecturer completed the semester by upgrading to a personally paid-for Zoom account and then uploading recordings of sessions onto the student platform. For the students, it was a frustrating experience. Anecdotal evidence indicated that several lecturers used their phones to talk about their slides. Not surprisingly, formal student feedback showed that students were extremely dissatisfied with their experience, and many requested a refund of their tuition fees. Lecturers who were deemed to be 'difficult' were simply not re-employed by the Institution for the next teaching session.

Institution 2

As noted earlier, lecturers were brought back to campus to deliver their material from fully equipped studio-lecture rooms. Instead of Zoom, which is a general-purpose, video-conferencing platform, the Institution used Blackboard Collaborate, which is a virtual classroom tool. All teaching and learning materials were uploaded to the student platform in real time. Each studio was equipped with tracking cameras and live-chat facilities. The end-of-trimester feedback from students indicated that the online learning environment strongly mirrored that of a face-to-face classroom. The overwhelming majority of students were very satisfied with their experience and about 90% stated that they would prefer to stay online in later teaching periods.

CONCLUDING REMARKS

For better or worse, online teaching is here to stay. One challenge is for educational institutions to invest in the required infrastructure. A second and more important challenge is for academics to be trained in and comfortable with technologies that support online education. Education providers should not rely on individual lecturers to effect the latter change.

REFERENCES

'It is not production quality that counts in Educational Videos- here's what students value most'. 2020. The Conversation at *https://theconversation.com/its-not-production-quality-that-counts-in-educational-videos-heres-what-students-value-most-151573* accessed 30 March 2021

Taleb, N. N. (2007). The Black Swan: the impact of the highly improbable. Penguin Books. London: UK.

https://deborahalupton.medium.com/timeline-of-covid-19-in-australia-1f7df6ca5f23 accessed 30 March 2020.

https://www.theage.com.au/national/victoria/standing-desks-monitors-sell-out-as-australia-starts-working-from-home-20200316-p54aiv.html accessed 30 March 2021.

Chapter

8

COVID-Driven Transition to Online Teaching: A Reflection

Syed Uddin, Universal Business School Sydney

ABSTRACT

'Face-to-face teaching has no effective substitute' has been a long-held belief within academia. However, the COVID-enforced transition to online delivery in early 2020 has cast doubt on the belief. This chapter contributes to the discussion by describing direct experience gained during the transition period. The author suggests that, because only a year has passed since the transition began, it is too early to be precise about the effectiveness of online versus onsite teaching. However, the experience so far is quite encouraging.

ONLINE TEACHING: INTRODUCTION

COVID-19 disrupted nearly everything that, for ages, the academic world had taken for granted. Time will tell whether history will judge this pandemic as a 'Black Swan' event (Taleb, 2007). However, there is no doubt that it has played a catalytic role in the widespread acceptance of online delivery as a viable substitute for face-to-face (F2F) teaching. Necessity paved the way for the world-wide emergence of online teaching, so it should not be considered as a 'disruptive innovation' event (Bower & Christensen, 1995).

Most providers of higher education were unprepared for the sudden move to online teaching. Hence, the speed at which many providers devised paths, established protocols, and built capacities to stay afloat during the public health emergency is simply astounding. For some, this capacity building was designed, not only to remain relevant, but also to take full advantage of the opportunity for process innovation provided by the pandemic and to expand their business.

THE UBSS CASE

The relatively young and exceptionally confident higher education provider, Universal Business School Sydney (UBSS), navigated through the 'choppy waters' very well. In fact, it adapted successfully to the changed environment within days. This might sound implausible to an external observer but was clearly apparent and understandable to those who watched it unfold in real-time and from a close range.

The success of UBSS was due to many factors, including the farsightedness, strong leadership and agility of the senior management and academic teams; appropriate earlier investment in online resources; a hardworking and talented technical and support staff; a knowledgeable, loyal, and dedicated teaching team (staff turnover at UBSS is exceptionally low); and excited and willing learners.

CHALLENGES AND MITIGATING STRATEGIES: PERSONAL

Fear of the unknown

For me, a cautious person, going online over-night was a daunting challenge. However, I had no choice but to meet the challenge head on and I had to muster the inner strength and courage to do so. I knew well that if 'I move beyond my fear, I shall feel free'

(Johnson, 1998). Within weeks I realised that the change was working in my favour.

Home office capacity

Following the onset of COVID-19, F2F sessions at all higher education providers in NSW ceased. I was working from home, but my home-office equipment was not designed to handle the heavy traffic associated with online classes, and delivery was initially unsatisfactory. However, the problem was solved very quickly as UBSS had already been developing purpose-built, on-campus lecture studios and these were up and running within days. All UBSS lecturers were then able to return to campus to deliver their lectures. The decision by management to install state-of-the-art studios proved to be a masterstroke.

Travelling to and from campus

When the NSW government placed a temporary ban on F2F teaching, it also advised persons aged 60 and above to avoid travel as much as possible. This created an extra layer of worry for those UBSS academics who were above the age threshold and were required to be onsite to deliver classes to students who were offsite. Seeing this as a potential 'blind spot', the UBSS academic leadership immediately drafted a letter explaining the reason for academic travel and advised the lecturing staff to carry the letter with them while commuting between home and campus. This was a simple step, but one that delivered much-needed peace of mind to lecturers.

Risk of contracting the virus on campus.

UBSS management wasted no time in transforming the campus to an official COVID-safe workplace, reducing to a minimum the risk of contracting the virus while being on campus.

CHALLENGES AND MITIGATING STRATEGIES: PEDAGOGICAL

Student engagement

Engaging with students in online classes poses difficulties since the students are not physically in the same room as the lecturer. I have been able to overcome these difficulties with a range of measures including careful selection of learning materials, flipping the classes and allowing / frequently inviting students at random to initiate discussion, organising students into break-out sessions, showing short videos, using humour and anecdotes, asking students for feedback, devising exciting and unpredictable beginnings for sessions, addressing students by their first name, and inviting students to connect the topic in hand with those of previous sessions.

Eye-contact and body language

The absence of these subtle but powerful cues in a digital teaching environment is challenging. I have been meeting the challenge by keeping my cameras live for the entire teaching period and frequently asking students to show their faces on screen while talking. I address students directly. I do not sit down while delivering lectures and I walk around the room as if I am getting closer to students in front of me.

Sustaining students' interest

The temptation for students to be distracted in a home environment is always present. I have been looking for clues from the presence or absence of sounds and I often make observations or frame questions like - 'How old is the baby'? 'It's nice music-what genre is it'? 'Is everything OK at home'? 'What is the weather like at your place'? I provide content-based quizzes in every session and give the students their scores immediately after the quiz. These tactics have been quite effective.

Academic integrity issues

Pre-emptive measures like nominating tight timeframes for completion of assignments, setting different questions for different students, and pairing students to work together have helped minimise integrity issues. For group assignments, I use confidential peer evaluation as part of the assessment of every student's contribution. In addition to these, UBSS has a clear and well-publicised plagiarism policy. Turnitin software and one-on-one support for referencing have been delivering favourable results.

Student accomplishment

There is concern that student outcomes associated with online delivery might be inferior to those from F2F learning. Interestingly, the performance of my students in the present digitalized environment has been the same as in the earlier sessions delivered F2F.

A careful selection and application of the approaches described above along with adoption of the strategies highlighted in the REMOTE framework (Israeli, 2020) can facilitate a win-win outcome with online delivery.

CONCLUDING REMARKS

Online teaching is neither a pure innovation nor a new direction. For several decades there has been a trend toward online teaching, and COVID-19 has simply accelerated this trend. Whether the present approach will be a short-lived circumstantial necessity or a serendipity, time alone will tell. However, it is implausible that when the pandemic is over, online teaching will again be sidelined.

I boarded the transition to online learning vehicle with apprehensions and I struggled with the approach during the first 2-3 weeks of implementation. However, I then become comfortable with online delivery and ended up winning the Dean's award for 'Outstanding Commitment to Teaching and Learning'. This is powerful testimony that in a conducive environment and with the right KSAs (knowledge, skills, and abilities) a desired outcome is possible irrespective of the mode of delivery.

REFERENCES

Bower, J. L., & Christensen, C. M. (1995). Disruptive Technologies: Catching the

Wave. Harvard Business Review. 73(1), 43-53.

Israeli, A. (2020). Digital learning REMOTE a framework for teaching online. Harvard Business Publishing accessed on 28 February 2021 from *https://hbsp.harvard.edu/inspiring-minds/remote-a-framework-for-teaching-online*

Johnson, S. (1998). Who Moved My Cheese? Putnam and Sons. New York: USA

Taleb, N. N. (2007). The Black Swan: the impact of the highly improbable. Penguin Books. London: UK.

Chapter

9

Never Lose the Moment

Art Phillips, Universal Business School Sydney

ABSTRACT

This chapter is woven from changes that occurred during the COVID-19 pandemic and which made remote teaching of students a necessity from the second quarter of 2020. The changes highlighted the need for academics to increase their awareness of student needs and to improve their teaching techniques to better meet these needs. The magnitude and pace of changes in the teaching environment since the onset of the pandemic have highlighted the need for a deeper understanding of student needs, clearer teaching, and better engagement.

CHANGE IS ESSENTIAL

The transition from face-to-face to online teaching, stemming from the global pandemic of COVID-19, has provided fresh visionary platforms for creatives, academics, and business entrepreneurs. Delivery of learning materials in the online environment cannot remain the same as classroom delivery, as lecturers now need to grab hold of each and every moment and nurture their student audience with continual engagement through heightening interest, introducing relevant surprise events, and allowing more fluid interaction through increased student participation.

Especially from 2020, we need to promote deeper learning engagement by developing student enthusiasm for online learning. Lecturers must recognize the necessity of being a star - a star of teaching, learning and engagement. They must step up to the plate and become this star. Knowing how to 'feel' the audience and being able to give them what they need on the spin of a dime are essential, even when there is not a soul in the room with the lecturer.

In this Chapter, I outline specific teaching techniques that I have acquired over many years as a lecturer in the higher education sector and an onstage performer in the entertainment industry and have honed during the COVID-19 induced switch to online delivery. These techniques produce more effective control of the audience, continually swaying them into wanting more and anticipating what is coming next on the content and showcase platter.

> **"Teachers need to integrate technology seamlessly into the curriculum instead of viewing it as an add-on, an afterthought, or an event." (Jacobs 2014).**

FROM CLASSROOM TO STAGE

The stage is where we now work, and a lecturer's repertoire needs to be on a conveyor belt, from which they pick items according to what the moment begs for. Having little learning titbits available at one's fingertips is crucial. Of course, the prepared lesson plan does not change much. What does change is how the lecturer delivers the story to engage learners more thoroughly by supplementing content with real-life personal examples. These examples must come from the heart, to help paint a more vivid picture of what is being taught.

Delivery requirements have changed. It is now essential to feel the room (feel your audience), in order to heighten student engagement and increase learning through enthusiastic student participation.

Lecturers need to have a refined charisma, like a pop artist on stage, if they are to grab their audience and give them the 'hooks' on which to hang their hats.

AWARDING MARKS FOR PARTICIPATION

Following the move to online delivery, I have increased attendance and participation in my postgraduate online class, 'Entrepreneurship Report', by using the following techniques:

Firstly, I have added two 5% random participation assessments. I take a pro-active approach to participation by providing the students with a stage, so to speak, on which they can shine in front of their audience (the class). Whether the student is extroverted or shy, this moves them into the spotlight, like a singer calling a fan onto the stage to participate in a musical performance. Their moment on the stage is important to them – we must not forget that, and we must actively encourage their participation.

Secondly, I now include three practical assessment activities in each trimester for each student (one every four weeks). These comprise 15-minute blocks dedicated to presentations. The content is an executive business summary, a marketing analysis with implementation skillsets, and a statement of the business finances with a focus on break-even calculations. The presentations provide a vehicle for the students to showcase their communication skills to other students and their lecturer. They also prepare students for the more challenging task of making professional presentations later to company shareholders, directors, and investment managers.

REAL-LIFE EXAMPLES

I also use various examples from my own entrepreneurial activities to supplement learning outcomes: audio files, visuals, music samples, real-life street stories, and in particular emotional 'wordsmithing' to help define and form useful marketing ideas.

Finding a parallel between subject content and an example from personal experience is golden, as it drives the storyline deeper for more entrenched learning memory and better life-long recall.

As stated by Dr. Christine Greenhow, Associate Professor of Educational Psychology and Educational Technology at Michigan State University: *"Online learning can be as good or even better than in-person classroom learning. Research has shown that students in online learning performed better than those receiving face-to-face instruction, but it has to be done right. The best online learning combines elements where students go at their own pace, on their own time, and are set-up to think deeply and critically about subject matter combined with elements where students go online at the same time, interacting with other students, their teacher, and content, and getting feedback".*

Facilities to teach online must be state-of-the-art, embracing seamless audio, visual and presentation technology. This is the situation at UBSS, which spent considerable amounts of time and money to provide resources specifically for online delivery. The feel of a well-designed television studio / lecture room is critical for lecturer enthusiasm and student engagement.

CONCLUSION

Engagement is everything. Real learning evolves from engagement. Online learning is not for students slouching in chairs; they must be alert and engaged during every moment of a lecture.

As recording artist Barry Manilow stated to Art and the band: *"Collecting my thoughts for a short period of time prior to walking on the stage is critical. To understand the importance of connecting with your audience and keeping every moment special and interactive once you are in front of your audience is vital"* (Manilow 1983).

Art Phillips was the recording and touring guitarist for Barry Manilow during 1981 ~ 84, performing over 150 concerts in the USA, Japan, Australia and globally. They performed at the Royal Albert Hall London to Prince Charles and Princess Lady Diana Spencer (1983), and on August 27, 1983 they also performed on the grounds of Blenheim Palace, the ancestral home of the Duke of Marlborough where Winston Churchill was born. This event was an outdoor summer concert, like Woodstock, with an audience of over 50,000 people. The Duke and Duchess were fans of Manilow, which made the arrangements possible. This concert marked the first time such an event ever occurred at the Palace.

> **I close with a statement I made while delivering a paper at a conference in Los Angeles in 2017: "Never lose your audience, as once you do it's all over" (Phillips 2017).**

REFERENCES

Greenhow, C. 2018, posted 2020, *https://www.sciline.org/covid-expert-quotes/online-learning#q1*

Jacobs, H, 2014, *https://elearningindustry.com/inspirational-elearning-quotes-for-elearning-professionals*

Manilow, B. 1983, personal statement to his touring band

Phillips, A 2017, conference on music production libraries: The 4M's, Los Angeles CA USA, October 2017

Chapter

10

New Virtual Reality in Knowledge Transfer

Nilima Paul, Universal Business School Sydney

ABSTRACT

Although digital technologies have augmented the transfer of knowledge during the last decade, the COVID-19 restrictions and limitations have propelled this to a new height. Almost every facet of transferring formal knowledge has been forced to use digital technologies. This chapter draws on the author's experience at Universal Business School Sydney (UBSS), where COVID-19 has not only expedited the sharing of knowledge through virtual modes but has also helped create a new generation of educational tools. Time will tell whether financial imperatives will cause digitalisation to become the new norm, but current indications are that it will.

INTRODUCTION

With the unprecedented restrictions placed by COVID-19 on face-to-face (F2F) teaching, virtual delivery of lessons has become ubiquitous. Whilst virtual modes of delivering information have been around since the mid-1980s, it was not until the late 1990s that they became widely used. Since the onset of COVID-19, this use has skyrocketed. According to a UNESCO study, the total market value of digital learning rose from US$0.3b in February 2020 to US$1.3b in March 2020 and more than US$20b by October 2020. Annual investment in learning technology companies, which was negligible prior to 2016, is projected to rise from about $100b in 2020 to US$350b by 2025.

RATIONALE

While F2F delivery may still be the most effective and preferred mode of delivering lessons, virtual learning has been increasing in popularity. Various tertiary institutions have introduced distance learning for their students, primarily through postal supply of materials such as pre-recorded CDs, DVDs, and cassettes. However, distance learning is not necessarily virtual learning, which comprises delivery of learning materials online, mainly through the Internet. Virtual learning has many forms: Podcasting; videoconferencing; webinars; and online posting and accessing of materials. In recent years, webinars have become the most common form of virtual learning, due to rapid advancements in tele-communications technology and computer/smartphone devices.

REALITY

Virtual learning has many advantages over online learning including any-time access, self-paced learning, near-zero classroom costs, and the ability to communicate with large audiences across global boundaries. However, virtual learning also has limitations, such as exclusion of those who do not have access to the Internet, Wi-Fi or electric power; device breakdowns; time differences between teachers and students and among students; impersonality; cyber theft; IP issues; and most importantly the inability to mingle with other students and learn from the physical environment. Also, many hands-on, practical exercises cannot be effectively demonstrated or undertaken in virtual mode.

Progress in enhancing the quality of online learning has been accelerated by the COVID-19 pandemic. Academics now have at least one year's experience with online learning, most have enhanced their skills in online delivery, and many have substantially upgraded their digital access and equipment. Consider another aspect of virtual reality, namely international conferences, and meetings. COVID-19 has caused many of these to be held online, and numerous issues have been resolved and difficulties overcome by innovative, creative, and agile behaviour on the part of participants.

At UBSS, virtual classes were introduced immediately following the introduction of the COVID-induced regulations prohibiting F2F classes. My personal experience in delivering online classes since then indicated that:

- Attendance rate was low.
- Among students who did attend, most were busy doing other things and paid little or no attention to the material being presented and discussed.
- Since the students did not pay proper attention in the earlier class(es), it was difficult for them to absorb the material presented in following classes.
- Students did not interact effectively with each other.

THE FUTURE

Given the continuing uncertainty around the duration of the COVID-19 pandemic, and most importantly the possibility that further mutations of the COVID virus will pose more threats for, and place more pressures on, the education industry, it is almost certain that the virtual mode of learning will continue for some time. Educational institutions must prepare for this quickly, including providing appropriate software and physical infrastructure. Those that fail to do this can expect to lose students.

COVID-19 is a warning to the sector that it must be able to provide attractive and effective alternatives to the traditional modes of learning. It is arguable that, in the not-too-distant future, the fast rate of climate change and the increasing incidence of natural calamities will cause many F2F classes to be cancelled and, in those circumstances, the virtual mode will be an important substitute.

Virtual delivery can also facilitate the penetration of education and learning to all corners of the world.

CONCLUSIONS

This chapter has highlighted the importance of virtual learning and the need for institutions in the education sector to further sharpen their online capabilities and to invest in supporting infrastructure and equipment if education is to remain affordable, profitable, and sustainable. To facilitate this, it is recommended that:

- Structured surveys be undertaken to identify more clearly the bottlenecks in the existing system and provide suggestions for addressing these bottlenecks.
- Improved mechanisms be developed and introduced to ensure that students attend the online classes, so that they not only obtain academic qualifications but also impound information and skills from the subjects they are studying.
- The sector and its industries cooperate to ensure education's sustainability.

REFERENCES

https://www.weforum.org/agenda/2020/04/coronavirus-education-global-covid19-online-digital-learning

https://www.europeandataportal.eu/en/impact-studies/covid-19/education-during-covid-19-moving-towards-e-learning

Chapter

11

Some Effects of COVID-19 on the Higher Education Sector

Igor Bosma, Universal Business School Sydney

ABSTRACT

The onset of the COVID-19 pandemic has had a profound impact on all aspects of business and society. In the higher education sector, it triggered an immediate and total transition to offsite, mainly online, learning. This chapter considers the impact of the transition on the student learning experience, educational outcomes, teaching, and technological innovation, drawing on insights from across the sector including providers already well versed in online delivery strategies. The chapter also provides a broader stakeholder context that can inform strategies for the future 'new normal'.

INTRODUCTION

An incontestable truth is that the Coronavirus, which first became apparent to those outside China in early 2020, has profoundly affected everyone in a myriad of ways. In one year, an estimated 40,000 academic articles on the pandemic have been published worldwide (Allen, 2021). Complementing this is the ubiquity, diversity and incalculable quantum of comment and opinion outside of academia.

Education is one sector that has been and continues to be significantly affected, with many providers, both Vocational (VET) and Higher Education (HE) across numerous disciplines, required to transition away from face-to-face to online teaching or some other form of 'distancing' or hybrid model.

The forerunner to 'distance' education in Australia (and what is today TAFE Digital) has its genesis in response to another emergency, the typhoid epidemic of 1910. At that time, Sydney Technical College was contracted to convert old railway cars into classrooms that could be transported around NSW to deliver training to remote railway workers who were unable to travel to Sydney because of the epidemic (Latchem, 2017).

TRANSITION TO ONLINE LEARNING

In the wake of COVID-19, online learning was either mandated by or a consequence of various government edicts or was an operational response to the challenges imposed (NSW State Government, 2020).

TAFE Digital did not need to make significant changes to its front-end delivery strategy. The ramping up of back-end operations amounted largely to enabling teachers and administrative staff to work from home by providing them with delivery software for home-based operations such as Moodle, Equella, Student Administration System (SAM) and the new TAFE Digital Campus (TDC). TAFE Digital's systems and processes were deployed across the State's face-to-face network in conjunction with Zoom (initially), allowing remote delivery of classes to begin in early March 2020. Technical limitations and security issues with Zoom caused a rapid switch to Microsoft Teams' Online & Remote Classroom platform.

Universities also quickly established and implemented new protocols, ensuring little disruption to content delivery. Students and staff had to adapt too. Technology was ramped up quickly to accommodate operational requirements and provide foundational capability for increased future opportunities (UBSS Online). The latter included the establishment of lecture studios and support technologies.

ONLINE DELIVERY, BEST PRACTICE AND CONTEXT

Student attitudes toward online delivery are highly contextual and cohort dependent. If participation and completion rates, which are universally very low (5-10%) for traditional online delivery (Bawa, 2016), are indicative, then one might conclude that online learning is preferable to onsite learning, as participation rates at TAFE Digital doubled in the first full year of online learning. Nuance, however. moderates this observation as many free government-funded VET short courses (e.g., under JobMaker) were made available following the transition to online learning. Those accessing these free courses, which comprises most of the increase in enrolments during the year, have typically been recently retrenched and are strongly motivated to re-enter the workforce. Many view the free courses as an opportunity to strengthen their CVs by obtaining formal status for skills they already possess. Adopting a socio-cognitive perspective, one would reasonably infer a high degree of self-efficacy in this cohort's ability to persist and self-regulate (Zimmerman, 1989) as a key contributor to the rise in participation rates.

Evening students studying Marketing at TAFE Meadowbank preferred online over face-to-face learning (Vox-Populi, 2020). Many were studying after work and lived across a relatively large geographic area. Finishing at 9pm made this a very attractive option for both students and teachers. Engagement (measured by attendance and confirmed by completions) was higher. Learning styles (VARK model) appear to be a significant factor in driving learning preferences (Miller, 2021). Interestingly and perhaps somewhat counter-intuitively, the author viewed research which found that, in one sector in the United States, just over half (55%) of all students strongly preferred face-to-face learning (Miller,

2021). Whether a year of lockdowns (or lockups) and the significant curtailment of other freedoms caused by COVID-19 was a causal factor is not stated.

My experience across a range of teaching and student contexts (low- and high-level VET to post-graduate HE) and cohort attributes across a range of providers concurs with much of the research, once synthesised and contextualised. Fundamentally, learning delivery mode preference is highly situational (Saxena, 2021). For example, I interviewed one student whose preferences varied across different study areas and life-cycle stages. As a young university engineering student with ostensibly no responsibilities other than to herself, face-to-face learning complemented by the socialisation of university campus life was extremely important. Later, as a mother working full-time and undertaking dual diplomas in Project and Leadership Management (hitherto unavailable widely online), only online learning was feasible. Options in the form of tutorial support and flexible ad-hoc class attendance were also indicated. Flexibility is undoubtedly the key. The increase in online delivery capability has evidently widened the market.

STAKEHOLDER CONTEXT, RISK AND OPPORTUNITIES

The Australian 'sandstone' university model has arguably been broken for some time, with the coronavirus pandemic merely providing illumination of the situation. The model depends heavily on cashed-up foreign students funding dubious research and increasingly cross-subsidising a range of courses with educational outcomes of questionable value. It is being undermined by cultural problems, notably the encroachment on free speech. Under this paradigm, administration and bureaucracy have flourished while teaching and research capability have diminished (Spartacus, 2021). Coupled with an increasingly radical revisionist approach to an ever-widening curricula rejecting Western enlightenment, which has now metastasised beyond the humanities, one is left to ponder what differentiating factors will attract foreign students to a 'Western' education. This self-inflicted gap presents a significant opportunity for second and third tier HE providers to provide an educational experience with an 'Australian flavour'.

Current risks associated with the heavy reliance on foreign students centre around government policy and immigration rules governing the visas that may be granted to potential and current students. The availability of different visa categories is a matter of government policy. Certain visa categories favour those who possess skills where critical shortages have been identified, with these categories being subject to on-going review. The granting of permanent residency (PR) has also been made more restrictive since 2017. For example, those with accounting degrees now must meet a higher threshold before permanent residency is granted (International Student Support, n.d.).

Australia has a favourable and improving political environment in terms of stability, freedom from corruption, and accountability of government, ranking 10th (out of 180 countries) on the Global Corruption Index in 2020 (up from 15th place in 2019) (Global Corruption Index, 2020). The Government's response to the pandemic has included the prevention of international travel from a range of countries that have traditionally been the leading catchment area for foreign students, namely China, India, and Nepal. Currently, there is considerable uncertainty about when the traditional business model, incorporating active student acquisition and face to face delivery, can recommence (International Student Support, n.d.).

Some political actors (e.g., China's Communist regime) continue to portray Australia as a 'racist' and 'dangerous' country. Paradoxically, they claim that Australia's lack of action on 'climate change' will deter potential foreign students from China and elsewhere. This 'fake news' narrative for political purposes is, not infrequently, promulgated by certain sections of the local media, also for political purposes (Hunter, 2020). This is in stark contrast to the results of international student surveys, which consistently yield responses that are overwhelming positive, with overall satisfaction levels of around 90% for students (VET and HE).

Further, 75% of students surveyed in the International Graduate Outcomes Survey (2018) stated that Australia was their first choice for overseas study. In addition, ongoing significant support exists for foreign students in Australia (COVID-19 and Beyond for International Students, n.d.).

CONCLUSION

These largely foundational aspects present an overall positive outlook for Australia's export of higher education. However, it is imperative that VET and HE providers continue to exploit Australia's natural and structural advantages and publicise these among stakeholders (How to engage us, 2021). Within the sector, there is an opportunity for second and third tier providers to gain market share by focusing on traditional benefits of Western education. It is auspicious and timely that key stakeholder representation appears to be widening (GCA Chair and CEO Alan Manly Appointed to MACSM, 2021). This not only protects the legacy of quality education, but it also permits opportunities presented by the Coronavirus pandemic to be leveraged in the 'new-normal' education industry.

REFERENCES

Allen, D. W. (April 2021). Covid Lockdown . A Critical Assessment of the Literature, 2.

Anonymous. (2020, June 3). My University's Betrayal of Truth. Quadrant.

Bawa, P. (2016, March). Retention in Online Courses. SAGE Publishing, p. 1.

COVID-19 and Beyond for International Students. (n.d.). Retrieved from Study Australia: *https://www.studyinaustralia.gov.au/English/student-support*

GCA Chair and CEO Alan Manly Appointed to MACSM. (2021, April). Retrieved from Universal Business School Sydney: *https://www.ubss.edu.au/articles/2021/april/gca-chair-and-ceo-alan-manly-appointed-to-macsm/*

Global Corruption Index. (2020). Retrieved from Transparency International Australia: *https://transparency.org.au/global-ranking/*

How to engage us. (2021, April 22). Retrieved from Department of Home Affairs: *https://www.homeaffairs.gov.au/help-and-support/how-to-engage-us/committees-and-fora/ministerial-advisory-council-on-skilled-migration*

Hunter, F., & Bonyhady, N. (2020, January 14). Bushfires pose costly risk to Australia's booming international education market. The Sydney Morning Herald.

International Graduate Outcomes Survey. (2018). Retrieved from Department of Education, Skills and Employment: *https://internationaleducation.gov.au/research/Pages/Data-and-Research.aspx*

International Student Support. (n.d.). Retrieved from Study Australia: *https://www.studyinaustralia.gov.au/English/student-support*

Latchem, C. (2017). Using ICTs and blended learning in transforming technical and vocational education and training. Commonwealth of Learning, 85.

Miller, C. (2021, February 23). Why Learning Preferences Are More Important Than Learning Styles. Retrieved from BIZ Library: *https://www.bizlibrary.com/blog/learning-methods/learning-preferences-versus-learning-styles/*

NSW State Government. (2020, March 23). Retrieved from Restrictions begin as schools move towards online learning: *https://education.nsw.gov.au/news/latest-news/restrictions-begin-as-schools-move-towards-online-learning*

Saxena, B. (2021, April 19). Learning Mode Preference. (I. Bosma, Interviewer)

Spartacus, S. (2021, March 13). Sydney University choses to chase cash, not quality. The Spectator.

UBSS Online. (n.d.). Retrieved from Universal Business School Sydney: *https://www.ubss.edu.au/ubss-online/*

Vox-Populi, T. (2020, November 4). Class Mode Delivery Preference. (I. Bosma, Interviewer)

Zimmerman, B. J., & Schunk, D. H. (1989). Self-Regulated Learning and Academic Achievement. New York: Springer.

Chapter

12

Academic Integrity in an Online World: A COVID-19 Perspective

Wayne Smithson, Universal Business School Sydney

ABSTRACT

The Covid-19 induced switch to online teaching and the associated move to offsite assessment have increased the opportunities for students to cheat. The main forms of cheating include plagiarism and contract cheating for coursework and using an impersonator in exams. This chapter identifies the reasons why students cheat and considers how offsite cheating can be reduced by improved assessment design and increased awareness.

THE MAIN CAUSES OF CHEATING

It is widely accepted that many higher education students cheat in their assessments. The incidence of such misconduct has been quoted in the press at 6-10% (Sydney Morning Herald, 2019) but the percentage may be even higher in the private-provider sector where the academic motivation of students may be lower and institutional resources are less.

The burning question is: Why do students cheat? The Tertiary Education Quality and Standards Agency (TEQSA), Australia's quality assurance and regulatory agency for higher education, cites three key reasons: Opportunity (the ready availability of opportunities to cheat), Second Language (the increased difficulties of studying in a second language), and Teaching (dissatisfaction with the quality of teaching) (Bretag, 2016). Donald Cressy, a criminologist, explained the causes of cheating in terms of a Fraud Triangle, with the three sides of the triangle being Opportunity, Pressure (also known as incentive) and Rationalisation (sometimes referred to as justification) (Cressey, 1952).

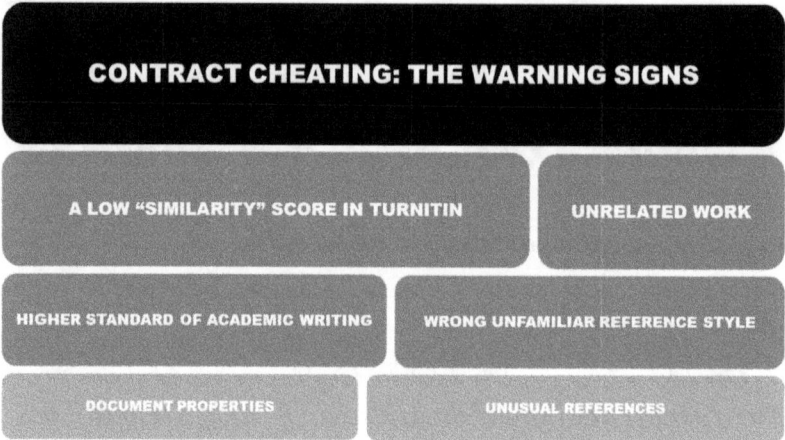

CONTRACT CHEATING: THE WARNING SIGNS

A LOW "SIMILARITY" SCORE IN TURNITIN	UNRELATED WORK
HIGHER STANDARD OF ACADEMIC WRITING	WRONG UNFAMILIAR REFERENCE STYLE
DOCUMENT PROPERTIES	UNUSUAL REFERENCES

Source: Bretag, 2020

It is noteworthy that Opportunity is the first element included in both the Bretag and Cressy classifications. The move to on-line assessments following the outbreak of the COVID-19 pandemic in early 2020 increased considerably the opportunity for students to cheat, due mainly to the removal of onsite invigilation.

"One of the problems of our society is that we spend too much time thinking about punishment and not enough about prevention." - Roy Hattersley

THE MAIN APPROACHES TO MINIMIZING CHEATING

A recent TEQSA seminar suggested that the key elements of an effective strategy to reduce cheating are Prevention, Identification (or Monitoring) and Action (Control through e.g., punishment). A toolkit developed by TEQSA (Bretag, 2020) focuses on the traditional responses of Identification and Action. However, these are at best reactive approaches to correcting poor behaviours. Also, the emphasis on Discovery and Punishment adds a significant administrative burden (and therefore cost) to the education providers, which ultimately must be passed on to students, most of whom do not cheat.

While it is accepted that Identification and Punishment are necessary components of a cheating-reduction strategy, the author's personal experience as a lecturer during the 2020 transition to online learning suggests that the most effective approach is Prevention. The following discussion reviews two aspects of Prevention, namely modifying assessment design and increasing awareness.

Modifying assessment design

The opportunity for students to engage in contract cheating or to arrange for another person to take an exam in their place can be reduced by chunking of assessments, reducing the weights of individual assessments, using unique case-based assessments, and including lecturer-student communication in assessments. The first three measures increase the cost-per mark of using outside resources to assist with the assessment and the last increases the benefit to students of preparing written answers themselves.

Chunking of assessments. This is a methodology that breaks assessments into small sections. (It may also be applied to teaching, with subjects being broken into small segments separated by activities and student /lecturer interaction.) A typical approach would be to replace a standard assessment with several smaller online assessments at short intervals.

Reducing the weights of individual assessments. This method increases the number of assessments so that the weight of every non-invigilated assessment is reduced to a level that discourages the student from incurring the effort and cost of identifying, contacting, communicating with, and paying a third party to undertake the assessment. A modification of this approach for a group assignment is to divide the assessment into a collective component and an individual component and spread the total mark over both components. While a group of students may be prepared to outsource an assignment worth 20 marks, they will be less willing to do so if the outsourced component carries only 10 marks. This approach also has the advantage of individualizing the potential assessment for each student, making identification of potential cheating easier.

Unique case-based assessments. Basing assessments on case studies rather than generic issues increases the cost to third parties of providing quality answers. This advantage is enhanced if the case studies are not widely known and have not be used by the lecturer in previous assessments.

One-on-one assessment. Including a one-on-one interaction between the lecturer and student as part of the assessment, e.g., via a scheduled Zoom meeting, allows the lecturer to identify the student and then, via questioning, assess their understanding of the methodology and content of any written answers. This supports mainly the Identification and Action (Punishment) approach to reducing cheating, but also contributes to Prevention, since students are more likely to undertake a written assignment themselves if they must defend it later.

Increasing awareness

Students are less likely to cheat if they are aware of the likelihood and consequences of being caught. They are more likely to be caught if all lecturers including especially new, casual lecturers are aware of traditional and new ways of detecting cheating and of the types of evidence required to determine cheating. New and better technologies are being developed in response to the rise in popularity of online teaching, but lecturers must be aware of these if they are to increase their identification of cheating. At UBSS, a Daily Bulletin is made available to all staff before the working day commences. This Bulletin keeps staff up to date with internal and external developments that might impact on their role within the institution, including assessment.

Students also need to be made aware that the institution's identification processes are effective and that penalties are being imposed on students deemed to have cheated. This information can be communicated by lecturers when they are discussing assessments with students.

> **"Intellectuals solve problems, geniuses prevent them" - Albert Einstein.**

CONCLUSION

The TEQSA classification of the causes of and responses to cheating in assessments lends itself to a 3 x 3 matrix approach, with the three main causes of cheating being:

- Opportunity.
- Studying in a Second Language.
- Dissatisfaction with Teaching.

The three responses being:

- Prevention.
- Identification.
- Action.

This chapter focused on the Opportunity-Prevention cell of the matrix. It notes that the transition to online learning has been accompanied by an increase in the Opportunity to cheat. It suggests that the best response to this is Prevention, both by redesigning assessments and by increasing awareness among staff and students of approaches that are available and are being adopted to reduce cheating.

REFERENCES

Bretag, T. & Mahmud, S. (2016). (n.d.). A conceptual framework for implementing exemplary academic integrity policy in Australian higher education, Chapter 32 in Handbook of Academic Integrity (Ed. Tracey Bretag), Springer.

Bretag, T. Curtis, G. Slade, C. McNeill, M. (2020) https://www.teqsa.gov.au/academic-integrity-toolkit.

Cressey, R. (1952). Application and verification of the differential association theory. The Journal of Criminal Law, Criminology, and Police Science . PP, 43 – 52.

Singhal, P. (2019), Cheating found at UNSW up by 2000% as new detection methods used.

Sydney Morning Herald, 24th August 2019

Chapter

13

Online Proctoring: The Likely Future of Assessment

Jotsana Roopram, Universal Business School Sydney

ABSTRACT

The move to online learning caused by the COVID-19 pandemic has required higher education institutions to explore new and different strategies for assessing student performance. This has led to increased use of proctoring software in assessments. This chapter explores the advantages and disadvantages of proctoring software and the inevitable adoption of online proctoring as the future of assessment in Australia.

INTRODUCTION

The speed at which most higher education institutions adapted their practices following the onset of COVID-19 was impressive, particularly the abrupt move to online classes and associated online assessments. In early 2020, at the beginning of the transition period, many institutions chose the most cost-effective and user-friendly quick-fix vehicles for assessment, such as Moodle and other familiar student management systems and learning management platforms. However, some institutions also explored online proctoring – a service that allows students to take their exams in their own homes while being supervised either by a human invigilator online or by artificial intelligence software (or a combination of both) via a webcam and screen-sharing capability.

The higher education regulator and professional accreditation bodies in Australia did not impose mandatory requirements on assessments at the start of the pandemic. They were supportive of, and flexible with, assessment strategies employed by various institutions, provided that academic integrity and a positive student academic experience were driving factors in the decision-making processes and that the strategies chosen by the institutions were regarded as temporary while other options were being explored.

A SHIFT TO PROCTORING TOOLS AND ASSOCIATED CONCERNS

In 2020, several Australian universities, such as the Australian National University and the University of Queensland, seeking to retain the integrity of face-to-face supervised exams, announced plans to use online-proctoring software such as ProctorU and Proctorio (Currey, 2020). This decision was met with apprehension and criticism from many students, academics, and privacy experts, who expressed concerns about online proctoring, including:

- Proctoring software is *invasive and accusatory*. The legitimacy of this concern must be considered in light of the following question: Is being seated in a physical exam venue under constant surveillance from human invigilators less invasive than the use of proctoring software during an online exam?
- *Proctoring is inequitable*. Students need access to WI-FI and other technologies such as webcams, microphones, and speakers, as well as spaces that are quiet and free of interruption. However, with the world literally moving online, it is hard to imagine that students do not already have the technology needed to meet the requirements of online proctoring.
- Online proctoring *encourages unlawful use and distribution of data storage*. It should be noted that the proctoring software companies, and ProctorU in particular, meet privacy-legislation and industry-standard security requirements.
- Some students *lack confidence with technology*, and this could be a significant disadvantage to their academic performance in proctored exams. This concern did not apply to UBSS

students, since online classes and assessment tasks using proctoring technology had already been adopted by the time exams were held.

At UBSS, a survey conducted in February 2021 showed that 88% of undergraduate and postgraduate students preferred to continue their studies online, confirming the notions that students at UBSS have embraced online technologies and are comfortable using them in their studies and exams.

There is now a wide range of proctoring software that can be used by institutions based on the assessment type and the individual needs of the institution. Artificial intelligence, human-invigilated online proctoring, or a combination of both can be used effectively.

ADVANTAGES OF PROCTORING TOOLS

There are many advantages associated with using proctoring tools to assess student performance, including:

- *A wider range of assessment questions*, by being able to access huge memory banks.
- *Reduced carbon footprint*, by eliminating the use of paper and student travel.
- *Replacing handwritten with typed answers*. In the current digital age, most students prefer to type rather than write, and academics find it easier to read typed rather than hand-written answers.
- *Saving of student time*, by not having students travel to exam venues as well as enabling students to avoid the stressful logistics required before they are seated for face-to-face exams (Dimeo, 2017).
- *Authentication* (student identity is verified before the commencement of the exam).
- *Lockdown* (access to documents and notes, websites, and other software can be blocked for closed book exams).

- *Effective monitoring*, with strict exam conditions being maintained using the microphone and webcam (Dawson, 2021).

HEIGHTENED USE OF TECHNOLOGY

The increased use of technology is beneficial for students undertaking higher education. Even pre-COVID, the world was heavily dependent on technology, and those students who had not embraced it or were not comfortable with it were considerably disadvantaged. The pandemic-induced move to at-home work and online meetings and the widespread acceptance of these will generate, post-COVID, a demand for even greater familiarity with technology in almost every job market. Students participating in online assessments are being exposed to technologies that better equip them to meet these demands.

COVID-19 has revived a common and highly controversial question in higher education: Are face-to-face exams an outdated approach to summative assessment? While no assessment approach (face-to-face or online) can stop cheating and other forms of academic misconduct completely, use of the latest online proctoring tools can dissuade students from doing so, and therefore strengthen the integrity of the assessment process in general.

REFERENCES

Currey, E. (2020). Australian Universities should think twice before installing spyware on students' computers. The Strategist. Retrieved from *https://www.aspistrategist.org.au/australian-universities-should-think-twice-before-installing-spyware-on-students-computers/*

Dawson, P. (2020). Strategies for using online invigilated exams. Retrieved from: *https://www.teqsa.gov.au/sites/default/files/strategies-for-using-online-invigilated-exams.pdf?v=16037580322*

Dimeo, J. (2017). Online exam proctoring catches cheaters, raises concerns. Inside Higher Ed. Retrieved from *https://www.insidehighered.com/digital-learning/article/2017/05/10/online-exam-proctoring-catches-cheaters-raises-concerns*

Chapter

14

Reducing Students' Technostress in Online Classes: Three Technical Methods

Arash Najmaei, Independent consultant

Zahra Sadeghinejad, Universal Business School Sydney

ABSTRACT

Technostress refers to the stress that is induced by using information and communication technologies (ICTs). It leads to depression, anxiety, fatigue, and reduced productivity. Online teaching and learning and their reliance on information technologies bring about technostress in students. In this chapter, the authors discuss three technical methods, namely interactive unit design, gamification, and multi-media content, that can help educators reduce students' technostress.

TECHNOSTRESS AND ONLINE TEACHING AND LEARNING

What is technostress and how does it relate to teaching and learning? According to Ragu-Nathan, Tarafdar, Ragu-Nathan, and Tu (2008, p. 418), technostress is the "stress experienced by individuals due to the use of ICTs". Brod (1984), who coined the term over four decades ago, described technostress as a modern disease of adaptation caused by an inability to cope with new computer technology in a healthy way. Over the last few years, the so-called technology-enhanced learning (TEL) methods, including mobile learning, blended learning, synchronous learning, online tutoring and massive online open courses, which have been facilitated by new technologies such as learning analytics, intelligent tutoring systems and various learning applications, have prompted higher education institutions to increase their investment in new teaching and learning (T&L) technologies (Al-Abdullatif, 2020; Kebritchi, 2017; Upadhyaya, 2020; Wang, 2020b).

The proliferation of new T&L technologies provides not only myriads of opportunities to support teaching and learning, but also creates numerous challenges and sources of stress to technology users in higher education (Qi, 2019). As a result, technostress has become an important topic in the education literature (Qi, 2019; Wang, 2020a; Wang, 2020b).

The COVID-19 pandemic precipitated an extensive transformation of the global education landscape, supported by accelerated implementation of new integrated ICT solutions such as Zoom and Microsoft Teams. The pressure to adopt these new technologies can induce technostress in students which, if not managed properly, can have severe detrimental effects on their experience with online learning and consequently on the success of the ongoing transformation of learning delivery.

The purpose of this chapter is to discuss a series of proven techniques that can be easily adopted by educators to reduce students' technostress in online classes. In what follows, we first explain the methods and design of the research used to identify these techniques. We then discuss the techniques and their pedagogical implications.

METHODS AND DESIGN

Because teaching is a reflective practice (Loughran, 2016) we adopted a research-diary method for our research (Nadin, 2006).

We summarised, categorised, and analysed notes taken by two university lecturers on their individual experiences as online teachers during the COVID-19 pandemic. Reflexivity research is a difficult process and varies according to the tacit metatheoretical commitments of the researcher (Nadin, 2006). We used two diaries to minimize bias and cross-validate findings. We identified six techniques and classified them into two groups, namely technical techniques, and teaching techniques. In this chapter, we enumerate three technical techniques that can reduce students' technostress.

Interactive unit design

Interactive unit design follows the three-phase model of Initiation, Response and Feedback (IRF). Initiation (I) is generated by the teacher in the form of a question; Response (R) comes from the student when they answer the question; and Feedback (F) is provided by the teacher following the student's response (Duran, 2016). Designing lectures to be interactive using techniques such as Q&A zoom sessions, quizzes and flipping classes increases both the confidence of students and their ability to cope with the stress caused by the pressure to adapt to a fully online learning environment (Stone, 2019). Interactive design should be used in both synchronous and asynchronous classes because encouraging interactivity using discussion boards, blogs and other media increases student engagement and improves their time management (Stone, 2019). As noted by Park and Choi (2009, p. 215), online courses must be designed for 'active participation and interaction' with academic and technical support embedded within the curriculum, 'taking into account the nature and diversity of the cohort and their particular needs when designing the unit' (Kuiper, 2015).

Gamification

The term "gamification" refers to the application of game mechanisms in non-gaming environments with the aim of enhancing the processes enacted and the experience of those involved (Caponetto, 2014). Gamification creates an enjoyable learning atmosphere by generating an environment where students can learn new content, perform new tasks, and practice skills learned while having a game-like experience (Osatuyi, 2018). Some popular gamification applications that have been widely used in the education sector and can help educators reduce students' technostress are: 1) Gimkit, 2) Class Dojo, 3) BookWidgets, 4) Classcraft, and 5) Kahoot. Huang and Soman (2013) offer a five-step approach for implementing gamification in online classrooms: Step 1) Understanding the students' learning requirements and the context of the subject. 2) Defining learning objectives for gamified tasks. 3) Structuring the experience by breaking down the learning points and defining rules of the game, 4) Identifying resources required to use the game such as time, money, and system requirements, and 5) Applying the gamification tools.

Multi-media content

Multi-media content is important for online teaching (Al-Abdullatif, 2020; Albrahim, 2020). In this context, multimethod content refers to the use of multi-media and multi-format content such as recorded videos, power point presentations, vlogs, and podcasts. Multi-media content is educational, entertaining, and compatible with a wide range of learning styles (Ramlatchan, 2020). It helps students learn new content in a psychologically relaxed atmosphere suited to their individual preferences (Martin, 2019). As a result, a multi-method approach to online teaching and learning can reduce students' technostress. This was supported by notes from the diary for the Quantitative Methods and Strategic Management classes where teachers used a mix of media.

CONCLUDING REMARKS

The main pedagogical implication of this chapter is that, although student's technostress is inevitable, there are simple techniques that are readily available and are being used to reduce it. The explicit role of faculty managers and executives in supporting the implementation of these techniques cannot be ignored. Policies and organisational procedures must be put in place to help educators develop the capacity to use these techniques in their classes.

REFERENCES

Al-Abdullatif, A. M., Alsubaie, M. A., & Aldoughan, E. A. (2020). Exploring the Effects of Excessive Texting Through Mobile Applications on Students' Technostress and Academic Writing Skills in the Arabic Language. IEEE Access, 8, 166940-166950. doi:10.1109/access.2020.3024021

Albrahim, F. A. (2020). Online Teaching Skills and Competencies. The Turkish Online Journal of Educational Technology, 19(1), 9-20.

Brod, C. (1984). Technostress: The Human Cost of the Computer Revolu tion. Addison-Wesley, Readin.

Caponetto, I., Earp, J., & Ott, M. (2014). Gamification and education: A literature review. Proceedings of the European Conference on Games Based Learning, 1(1), 50-60.

Duran, D. (2016). Learning-by-teaching. Evidence and implications as a pedagogical mechanism. Innovations in Education and Teaching International, 54(5), 476-484. doi:10.1080/14703297.2016.1156011

Huang, W. H.-Y., & Soman, D. (2013). A Practitioner's Guide To Gamification Of Education. Report Series: Behavioural Economics in Action, 29(1), 1-39.

Kebritchi, M., Lipschuetz, A., & Santiague, L. (2017). Issues and Challenges for Teaching Successful Online Courses in Higher Education. Journal of Educational Technology Systems, 46(1), 4-29. doi:10.1177/0047239516661713

Kuiper, A., Solomonides, I., & Hardy, L. (2015). Time on task in intensive modes of delivery. Distance Education, 36(2), 231–245.

Loughran, J. J. (2016). Effective Reflective Practice. Journal of Teacher Education, 53(1), 33-43. doi:10.1177/0022487102053001004

Martin, F., Ritzhaupt, A., Kumar, S., & Budhrani, K. (2019). Award-winning faculty online teaching practices: Course design, assessment and evaluation, and facilitation. The Internet and Higher Education, 42, 34-43. doi:10.1016/j.iheduc.2019.04.001

Nadin, S., & Cassell, C. (2006). The use of a research diary as a tool for reflexive practice. Qualitative Research in Accounting & Management, 3(3), 208-217. doi:10.1108/11766090610705407

Osatuyi, B., Osatuyi, T., & de la Rosa, R. (2018). Systematic Review of Gamification Research in IS Education: A Multi-method Approach. Communications of the Association for Information Systems, 42. doi:10.17705/1cais.04205

Park, J. H., & Choi, H. J. (2009). Factors Influencing Adult Learners' Decision to Drop Out or Persist in Online Learning. Educational Technology and Society, 12(4), 207–217.

Qi, C. (2019). A double-edged sword? Exploring the impact of students' academic usage of mobile devices on technostress and academic performance. Behaviour & Information Technology, 38(12), 1337-1354.

Ragu-Nathan, T. S., Tarafdar, M., Ragu-Nathan, B. S., & Tu, Q. (2008). The consequences of technostress for end users in organizations: Conceptual development and empirical validation. Information systems research, 19(4), 417-433.

Ramlatchan, M., & Watson, G. S. (2020). Enhancing instructor credibility and immediacy in online multimedia designs. Educational Technology Research and Development, 68(1), 511-528.

Stone, C., & Springer, M. (2019). Interactivity, connectedness and 'teacher-presence': Engaging and retaining students online. Australian Journal of Adult Learning, 59(2), 146-169.

Upadhyaya, P., & Vrinda. (2020). Impact of technostress on academic productivity of university students. Education and Information Technologies, 26(2), 1647-1664. doi:10.1007/s10639-020-10319-9

Wang, X., Tan, S. C., & Li, L. (2020a). Measuring university students' technostress in technology enhanced learning: Scale development and validation. Australasian Journal of Educational Technology, 36(4), 96-112.

Wang, X., Tan, S. C., & Li, L. (2020b). Technostress in university students' technology-enhanced learning: An investigation from multidimensional person-environment misfit. Computers in Human Behavior, 105. doi:10.1016/j.chb.2019.106208

Chapter

15

Reducing Students' Technostress in Online Classes: Three Pedagogical Methods

Zahra Sadeghinejad, Universal Business School Sydney

Arash Najmaei, Independent consultant

ABSTRACT

Technostress refers to the stress that is induced by using technology. It leads to depression, anxiety, fatigue, and reduced productivity. Online teaching and learning and their reliance on information technologies produce technostress in students. In the preceding chapter, the authors discussed three technical methods, namely interactive unit design, gamification, and multi-media content, that can help reduce students' technostress. In this chapter, they discuss three teaching methods that can reduce students' technostress, namely support mechanisms (before and after class support, online and offline support), online inclusivity, and scheduled repetition.

TECHNOSTRESS AND ONLINE TEACHING AND LEARNING

In our earlier article, we defined technostress as the stress induced by one's inability to adopt new technologies (Ragu-Nathan, 2008). Technostress is a key dark side of technology and if not managed can act as a corrosive force with severe detrimental effects on one's productivity and psychological wellbeing (Bondanini, 2020; Brod, 1984). It has been established that online teaching and learning and the need to use a wide range of new technologies are a source of technostress among students (Wang, 2020).

The COVID-19 pandemic has created a new phase of online teaching in which a wider range of students has to adopt online technology. Consequently, increasing attention is being paid to methods and techniques that help educators reduce students' technostress (Qi, 2019; Upadhyaya, 2020; Wang, 2020). In Chapter 14, we elaborated on how we used a research diary technique (Nadin, 2006; Ohly, 2010) to extract three technical methods for reducing technostress. This chapter follows on with an illustration of three complementary pedagogical methods.

Support Mechanisms

The benefits of providing prompt and substantive support are well documented in the literature. Notes in our diary confirm these benefits. Mechanisms such as a mix of online and offline instructional consultation sessions (OICs) (Weay, 2012), before and after class consultations (Penny, 2004), online support communities such as WhatsApp groups, flipped classes where students learn by teaching others (Lewis, 2006), and connecting with students via online platforms such as Skype, telephone, email, and Zoom meetings, not only ensure that learners' needs are met more effectively but also increase teacher-learner interactions (Martin, 2019; Stickler, 2020). These result in a better experience for learners and a reduction in their technostress.

Online Inclusivity

It is well noted that students may feel isolated and disconnected in online courses, and this may affect how they adopt and use technologies to engage in class activities and learn new content (Kebritchi, 2017). The social constructionist view suggests that students and the community within which they interact socially cocreate their identities. Therefore, online students need to develop a shared sense of belonging, purpose, and norms in their online classes (Koole, 2014). An inclusive approach to teaching online classes is critical to achieving this goal.

Inclusive teaching involves active listening, creating an engaging learning atmosphere, emphasising students' uniqueness of identity, and ensuring that the students' need to belong is satisfied (Molbaek, 2017). A strong sense of identity along with belonging to and being a valued member of the knowledge community play a critical role in effective knowledge building and create the confidence and motivation required to adopt new technologies (Kebritchi, 2017). Therefore, a didactic approach to online inclusivity is a valuable method for reducing online students' technostress.

Scheduled Repetition

Research suggests that spaced or scheduled repetition of content improves memory, increases learning capacity, and reduces stress caused by the pressure to memorise and recall (Dumesnil, 2018). Ebbinghaus (2013)'s forgetting curve offers a theoretical explanation for the role of scheduled repetition in reducing students' perceived techno-stress. According to Ebbinghaus, the forgetting curve becomes less steep by each reminder indicating that the learner has a better chance of remembering for longer periods of time after each review (Dumesnil, 2018). This lessens technostress by reducing the reliance on and the demand for online technologies.

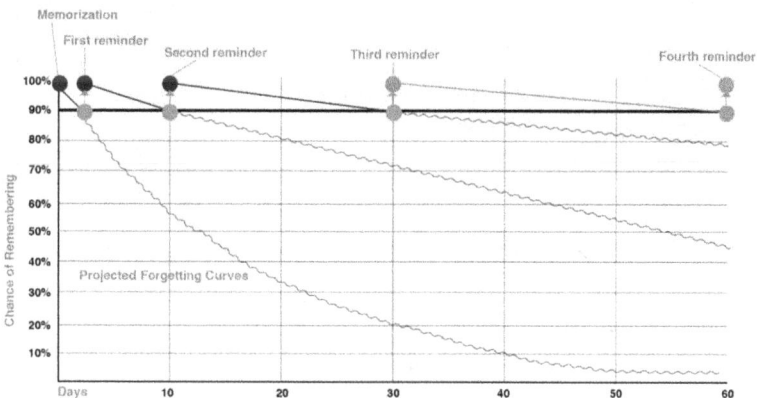

Ebbinghaus' Forgetting Curve

CONCLUDING REMARKS

As noted by Baran and Correia (2014), teachers "may feel uncertain, uneasy, and unprepared for the challenges of teaching online, lacking the tools and conditions they rely on to establish their expertise and teacher persona in the traditional classroom". Martin et al. (2019) suggested that the field of online learning research offers a ripe opportunity to contribute to both the practice of online instructors and the body of knowledge surrounding effective online learning. Specifically, in the wake of the COVID-19 pandemic, where more classes are being offered online and many teachers have no option but to teach online, learning about a repertoire of skills to use in online classes has significant implications for research and practice. Techniques that we discussed here may help teachers deliver online classes in ways that are less stressful for students and more conducive to learning.

Online teaching is the new normal in the world of education and technostress is an inevitable consequence of this phenomenon. Although online students may always suffer some degree of technostress, teachers can help them have a more pleasant online learning experience.

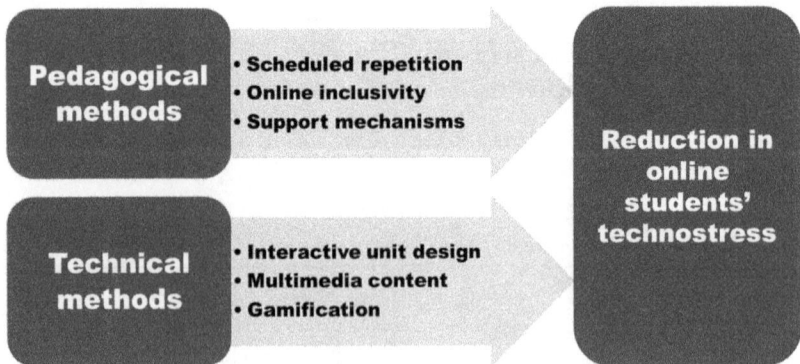

A schematic summary of methods to reduce online students' technostress

REFERENCES

Baran, E., & Correia, A.-P. (2014). A professional development framework for online teaching. TechTrends, 58(5), 95-101. doi:10.1007/s11528-014-0791-0

Bondanini, G., Giorgi, G., Ariza-Montes, A., Vega-Munoz, A., & Andreucci-Annunziata, P. (2020). Technostress Dark Side of Technology in the Workplace: A Scientometric Analysis. Int J Environ Res Public Health, 17(21). doi:10.3390/ijerph17218013

Brod, C. (1984). Technostress: The Human Cost of the Computer Revolu tion. Addison-Wesley, Readin.

Dumesnil, D. (2018). The effects of spaced repetition in online education. PhD dissertatio, Department of Electrical Engineering and Computer Science, Massachusetts Institute of Technology,.

Ebbinghaus, H. (2013). Memory: A contribution to experimental psychology. Annals of neurosciences, 20(4), 155-156.

Kebritchi, M., Lipschuetz, A., & Santiague, L. (2017). Issues and Challenges for Teaching Successful Online Courses in Higher Education. Journal of Educational Technology Systems, 46(1), 4-29. doi:10.1177/0047239516661713

Koole, M. (2014). Identity and the itinerant online learner. The International Review of Research in Open and Distance learning, 15(1), 52–70.

Lewis, C. C., & Abdul-Hamid, H. (2006). Implementing Effective Online Teaching Practices: Voices of Exemplary Faculty. Innovative Higher Education, 31(2), 83-98. doi:10.1007/s10755-006-9010-z

Martin, F., Ritzhaupt, A., Kumar, S., & Budhrani, K. (2019). Award-winning faculty online teaching practices: Course design, assessment and evaluation, and facilitation. The Internet and Higher Education, 42, 34-43. doi:10.1016/j.iheduc.2019.04.001

Molbaek, M. (2017). Inclusive teaching strategies – dimensions and agendas. International Journal of Inclusive Education, 22(10), 1048-1061. doi:10.1080/13603116.2017.1414578

Nadin, S., & Cassell, C. (2006). The use of a research diary as a tool for reflexive practice. Qualitative Research in Accounting & Management, 3(3), 208-217. doi:10.1108/11766090610705407

Najmaei, A., Sadeghinejad, Z. (2020). Reducing Students' Technostress in Online Classes: Three Technical Methods. UBSS Publications Series.

Ohly, S., Sonnentag, S., Niessen, C., & Zapf, D. (2010). Diary Studies in Organizational Research. Journal of Personnel Psychology, 9(2), 79-93. doi:10.1027/1866-5888/a000009

Penny, A. R., & Coe, R. (2004). Effectiveness of consultation on student ratings feedback: A meta-analysis. Review of educational research, 74(2), 215-253.

Qi, C. (2019). A double-edged sword? Exploring the impact of students' academic usage of mobile devices on technostress and academic performance. Behaviour & Information Technology, 38(12), 1337-1354.

Ragu-Nathan, T. S., Tarafdar, M., Ragu-Nathan, B. S., & Tu, Q. (2008). The consequences of technostress for end users in organizations: Conceptual development and empirical validation. Information systems research, 19(4), 417-433.

Stickler, U., Hampel, R., & Emke, M. (2020). A developmental framework for online language teaching skills. Australian Journal of Applied Linguistics, 3(1), 133-151. doi:10.29140/ajal.v3n1.271

Upadhyaya, P., & Vrinda. (2020). Impact of technostress on academic productivity of university students. Education and Information Technologies, 26(2), 1647-1664. doi:10.1007/s10639-020-10319-9

Wang, X., Tan, S. C., & Li, L. (2020). Measuring university students' technostress in technology enhanced learning: Scale development and validation. Australasian Journal of Educational Technology, 36(4), 96-112.

Chapter

16

Why the Student Voice Matters

Jotsana Roopram, Universal Business School Sydney

ABSTRACT

In today's digital world, expectations of the online experience and service include being quick, effortless, and convenient. There is also the demand to consistently meet high standards of professionalism and flexibility. The tech savvy generations live with and through technology. "Instant is expected", according to Jamieson (2018). The culture of accessing 'real time' information has prompted speedier services and higher expectations in an exceedingly competitive service-focused sector. Providing a personal, flexible, and seamless educational experience to students can give an institution the edge to not only remain relevant but also thrive in a constantly evolving and competitive industry.

INTRODUCTION

The student experience in Higher Education includes all aspects of their academic journey, including not only the academic study but also the social interactions on and off campus. Positive student experiences include allowing students to voice their concerns and communicate their needs. More importantly, positive student experiences also include institutions listening to these voices and acting (where possible) on the students' concerns.

While physical campuses still exist, face-to-face interactions that are not of the virtual kind are becoming increasingly rare and will probably remain so for the foreseeable future. Communication is an integral part of the student experience in today's online climate. Regular lines of communication with students must therefore be encouraged and maintained.

STUDENT FEEDBACK

Higher Education Institutions (HEIs) must stay engaged with students through a range of mechanisms including surveys and forums. Student feedback should be used to drive awareness. Action should be heavily reliant on these to provide real time attention. Post-service surveys (from online appointments with staff, live chats, and video calls) can be especially useful in providing instantaneous feedback for improvement or uncovering problems that require immediate consideration.

What sets Higher Education apart from other industries reliant on service is the duration of the 'transaction'. Students generally study at institutions for two to three years, a long period of time compared to purchasing a product in a store or enjoying a meal at a restaurant. HEIs must provide and sustain a positive experience for the duration of the student's journey. This is a challenging but not impossible task. According to King and McCullough (2021) HEIs must consider and understand the student experience in the post COVID-19 period in three ways: the 'Learning experience', the 'Personalised experience' and the 'Customer experience'. This approach recognises that the student experience is not a carbon copy of the customer experience in the service industry. Being a student as 'customers' of a higher education provider is far more 'unique and multi-faceted'. Education cannot be viewed as a single transaction with a singular purpose. Qualifications are no longer simply the product that students seek.

STUDENT DISSATISFACTION IS BOTH DAMAGING AND COSTLY

Student dissatisfaction is more damaging and costly to education institutions than is incensed customers to any other industry. Satisfied students are critical to student retention and word-of-mouth marketing has a positive impact on business and student outcomes. This has become more marked since the start of the pandemic.

COVID-19 has steered institutions into an educational revolution with an increased reliance on a model predicated on face-to-face service and communication. Live streaming from campus has become the new academic experience and is likely here to stay. While this move to online classes and online exams was almost immediate, sufficient attention to the student experience was sadly not prioritised. This is evident in the Quality Indicators for Learning & teaching (QILT) data for 2020, which highlight how much Australian universities, in particular, have missed the mark in this crucial area.

According to the KPMG report (March 2021), in what will be a highly competitive sector, students will be "more self-actualising, better informed, more instrumental and deliberate in their choices". HEIs will have to constantly evolve and innovate to retain students and keep them engaged. Betts (2021) suggests that, 'It is a time when business continuity must address the student voice.'

STUDENTS AS CUSTOMERS

Now, more than ever, there is pressure on HEIs to cease treating students as simply 'numbers' and to acknowledge them as customers. The pandemic has brought to the surface that the way to keep students happy is to understand their circumstances in an evolving world and cater to those circumstances. HEIs need to optimise their practices taking into account the disruption that is now occurring in the sector. The reward for the institutions is more loyal, engaged, and satisfied students.

REFERENCES

Betts, M. (2021). The student voice has spoken: and our response is… *https://www.campusreview.com.au/2021/03/the-student-voice-has-spoken-and-our-response-is-opinion/*

Jamieson, A. (2018). Why higher education needs to adopt a customer experience. approach. *https://www.digitalpulse.pwc.com.au/why-higher-education-needs-customer-experience-approach/*

King, M. and McCullough, M. (2021). Student experience in the age of the customer. KPMG. *https://home.kpmg/au/en/home/insights/2021/03/student-experience-in-the-age-of-the-customer.html*

Chapter

17

Plugged in But Disconnected: Challenges in the 2020 Online Transition

Harry Tse, Universal Business School Sydney

ABSTRACT

While universities and colleges are celebrating their successful transition to online learning and citing "highest-ever student feedback", the abrupt shift has left many in the education industry feeling disconnected. Students are limited in their connections with each other and with their teachers, and staff are often left feeling isolated without the daily support of their peers. Confusion around policy within the workplace, as well as high demand for IT support and training, has led to a feeling of being overwhelmed and under supported. This chapter highlights the main challenges faced by the author as coordinator of a large postgraduate introductory economics course during the transition to online delivery and how (successfully or not) these challenges were met.

INTRODUCTION

The world had never been more isolated nor more connected than it is right now. Interactions that we had previously thought were impossible online are now totally virtual, and teams connect more on chat platforms than in real life. In the university sector, students and staff are grappling with this new way of interfacing and while some university newsletters seem to report *"improved student feedback"* (West 2021), the catastrophic effect that COVID-19, and the abrupt move to online learning, has had on staff, students, and procedures must be felt somewhere. So, despite what the reported statistics suggest, I wonder: how can we really know how students and staff are doing when we are not seeing them face to face? This chapter looks at the challenges faced in connecting with students and peers during the period of virtual learning.

BACKGROUND AND CHALLENGES

In mid-March 2020, the threat of the COVID-19 pandemic in Australia caused all non-essential services including those being provided by higher education institutions to cease. Academic teaching staff were informed that all classes would be shifted online, effective immediately. Suddenly, 'teaching staff of all backgrounds and ages [had] to prepare and deliver their classes from home, with all the practical and technical challenges this entails, and often without proper technical support' (Rapanta, 2020). Many of these staff had never received any training in online delivery and were forced to undergo the stress of rethinking their courses, planning new lessons, and trying to understand unfamiliar technology in an extremely short period of time, all with little knowledge of the benefits or limitations of the technology available. IT departments all over the country were inundated with troubleshooting problems, technical difficulties, and requests for support, all while trying to get new systems up and running. Support staff were rushed to create training modules for the thousands of staff in their institutions and to roll out new procedures. These occurred amidst massive job cuts, general confusion and lack of security and transparency at the institutional level.

DIRECT IMPACTS ON STUDENTS AND ACADEMICS

During all this upheaval, there is one question at the forefront of every teacher's mind: 'How are my students doing?' The juggling act of learning new technology from a distance, losing peer-to-peer connections, and in many cases facing job insecurity do not surpass the anxiety that teachers feel when they suspect their students are falling behind or becoming disengaged.

In some cases, the shift to online learning has seen unexpected benefits. Scull et al. have found that in their Education Department at Monash University, students are responding well to online learning, with over 50% reporting high or very high satisfaction (Scull, 2020). They credit the strong social connections that they are fostering online in the form of: "bring your pet to class day"; weekly mental health check-ins; asking students which dish they are cooking for dinner this week; and thus, embracing the messiness of home and university life colliding (Scull, 2020). This leads one to wonder whether the shift to online learning has improved teaching quality, or rather, has perhaps made us more aware of our students and their individual needs now that we are seeing them in personal settings. While this would certainly account for some of the reported improvements in the student experience, it also places an additional mental load on staff who are, for the most part, untrained in skills like mental first aid. Furthermore, the ability to drop into a peer's office and ask advice on a certain student's wellbeing, or any other matter about the course, has disappeared with the shift to online learning. The use of online chat platforms has become both a constant and somewhat invasive presence, while simultaneously cutting out the casual corridor conversations that staff rely on to learn, laugh, and feel supported.

Nevertheless, what might work in a department like Social Sciences or Arts may not work in Business Schools, which are 'typically characterised by large class sizes and a significant proportion of international students' (Barker, 2020). In these classes, where students are often already out of their comfort zones with English as their second language, away from their home country or attending class virtually from overseas, students are more likely to feel isolated. Amanda White at UTS highlights that 'International students studying in their home country may also be experiencing further disadvantage because they are not regularly speaking English with their classmates and general interactions they have when living in Australia, yet their assessments are required to be submitted in English' (White, 2020). White suggests that this creates the perfect storm for anxiety and academic dishonesty, with students simply unable to bear the strain.

Furthermore, 'COVID19 and its accompanying financial crisis have added to the pressure, with many students losing their source of employment and having to trade-off attending classes with finding paid work' (White, 2020). The well-known phenomenon of teaching to the blank screens of students unwilling to turn their cameras on hints at a worrying trend. Many students, suffering the burden of having to support themselves in a COVID19 world, are struggling to remain engaged in a single task at a time. Students have reported 'attending class' while working part-time jobs such as ridesharing or food delivery.

CONCLUSION

White further highlights that the shift to online learning has not been as smooth as reported in published metrics, and that there has been significant 'discourse in the national media and on student-run social media pages about the dissatisfaction with online learning (Chrysanthos, 2020). To date, there are 67 petitions on Change.org demanding reduction of university fees due to online teaching and COVID19' (White, 2020). These worrying observations contrast quite dramatically with the positive picture that the Student Feedback Surveys provide, and beg the question: "How are our students actually doing?"

REFERENCES

Rapanta, C., Botturi, L., Goodyear, P. et al. Online University Teaching During and After the Covid-19 Crisis: Refocusing Teacher Presence and Learning Activity. Postdigit Sci Educ 2, 923–945 (2020). *https://doi.org/10.1007/s42438-020-00155-y*

Scull, J. Phillips, M. Sharma, U. & Garnier, K. (2020) Innovations in teacher education at the time of COVID19: an Australian perspective. Journal of Education for Teaching, 46:4, 497-506, DOI: 10.1080/02607476.2020.1802701

Smith, E. K., & Kaya, E. (2021). Online University Teaching at the time of COVID-19 (2020): An Australian Perspective, 9(2). *https://doi.org/10.22492/ije.9.2.11*

West, A (2021), UBSS Dean's message #117, 21 April 2021.

White, A. (2020), "May you live in interesting times: a reflection on academic integrity and accounting assessment during COVID19 and online learning", Accounting Research Journal, Vol. ahead-of-print No. ahead-of-print. *https://doi.org/10.1108/ARJ-09-2020-0317*

Chapter

18

Work-Integrated Learning in Australian Higher Education: An (R)Evolutionary Paradigm Shift

Wayne Smithson, Universal Business School Sydney

ABSTRACT

The COVID-19 pandemic has had a profound effect on work practices in most business sectors and industries. This article provides an overview of the impact on the academic arena in Australia, focusing on the disruption to education delivery and the subsequent evolution of a new environment for Work-Integrated Learning. The author argues that the pandemic brought forward changes that would have occurred anyway and concludes that in the future advanced learning may be embedded in the workplace rather than the traditional classroom.

INTRODUCTION

The case for Work-Integrated Learning (WIL) and the transition to an online platform for its delivery during the COVID-19 pandemic is similar to that for night following day – i.e., it was a fait accompli. The question before COVID-19 was not if and how the shift to a more digitalized approach would occur, but when would it happen. In essence, the pandemic has been the catalyst for a radical change in the teaching and learning of WIL, a change that has been reactive rather than proactive.

As with many historical crises in the educational ecosystem, the COVID-19 pandemic invoked agility, transition, and adaptation among participants. What differs in this case was the timeframe in which the transition took place.

While the changes from the pandemic across the higher education sector in Australia are still playing out, some astute and agile independent and public providers have adapted quickly to the changing situation, providing supporting evidence for Darwin's theory of evolution through natural selection and adaptation (Darwin 1859). For example, Universal Business School Sydney (UBSS) has introduced an academic theatre-style approach (lecture studios) to course delivery, provided on-line interaction with lecturers, used digital tracking cameras, and recorded sessions to provide students with quick and easy access for revision of key topics. These innovations are providing students with a TED-style interactive experience. The changes in the delivery mode have also allowed consultation with the lecturer in private breakout rooms, where individual teams can discuss the lecture material.

WIL PRE-COVID-19

The concept of WIL had been firmly entrenched in the academia psyche and many course curricula prior to the pandemic. Several variations and hybrids of the theme had been developed, including:

- Internships, both paid /unpaid.
- Work-experience internships.
- WIL with practical business-problem solutions.
- Case study and scenario solutions.
- Simulations, both on-line and face-to-face.
- Industry mentors.

Of course, the above list is not exhaustive, and many other hybrids and combinations have been developed. It is important to note that the student interaction with industry or business players varies along an experiential continuum from a high degree of interaction (such as one-on-one mentorship) to minimal interaction (e.g., through case studies and class-based scenario involvement).

COVID 19 - THE SILENT DISRUPTOR

As with all innovative breakthroughs and adaptations, there is normally a catalytic event that gives rise to a "eureka" moment. In this instance the advent of the COVID-19 pandemic in early 2020 was such an event.

WIL had evolved over the years as a valuable adjunct to the curricula of many universities and private higher education providers, being incorporated as either core to the assessment process such as a capstone subject or as added credit to some studies, in particular MBA units. With many of the different forms of WIL, industry partners were engaged to weave the fibre of theory and class learning into the fabric of real business life.

The degree to which students are exposed to the skill-based component of business, and other elements of the business ecosystem such as culture, politics, and the logistical environment, impacts the efficacy of the WIL program being used (Moore, 1993). The author has labelled this element the *enrichment factor*. It varies according to the specific form adopted along the WIL continuum. It can be argued that this specific WIL element adds significantly to the depth of the acquired student awareness and enrichment of the student's experience within the real or simulated business ecosystem. This factor has a significant bearing on the efficacy of the program from the student's perspective.

However, the advent of the pandemic significantly disrupted the capacity and ability of educational providers to conduct face-to-face interactions among students, industry representatives and individual mentors at one level, and the various internship hybrids developed by providers with industry partners at another.

EVOLUTIONARY ADAPTATION

As in Darwin's theory of natural selection and adaptation (but without Darwin's long timeframe), COVID-19 changed, significantly and rapidly, the nature and importantly the individual interactive component of WIL for many providers and students. Unsurprisingly, the vehicle of choice for evolutionary change and bridging the implementation gap was the ubiquitous internet. Combined with other forms of technologically enhanced interaction platforms such as Zoom, Microsoft Teams and Blackboard Collaborate, this quickly enabled not only the evolution of the virtual classroom but also the reach and enrichment factor of WIL programs.

It is important to note that, prior to the pandemic, many of these platforms were basic in their form and somewhat unrefined. However, this changed with the increased focus on, and heightened involvement in, the delivery mechanism not only in academia but also in the commercial office space. An incremental innovation tsunami for these platforms quickly ensued.

BUSINESS SIMULATION GAME AT UBSS

The Business Simulation Game (BSG) has been adopted by UBSS to further develop both the cognitive and analytical skills provided in all units of the School's degree programs. It is a commercial strategy and decision-making based virtual company game, which requires competing teams of students to analyse a range of business information across key specific areas in a global manufacturing company assigned and registered to the teams. The students formulate business strategies and make decisions relating to their virtual company across several distinct departments such as production, human resources, marketing, and finance. Importantly the students are accountable for their respective areas of responsibility and also for decision making and interpretation of market conditions.

Competition in the virtual global market is provided by the other teams enrolled in the game, who may be in the same class or in another school, state, or country. Given the global nature of the game there are sometimes as many 2,500 teams worldwide playing in a single game.

Every team's performance is assessed after each trading period or decision round (normally three rounds of operation). A series of computer-generated algorithms interpret the decisions and compare the output of each team allocated to the industry. This provides students with the opportunity to apply acquired theory and skills to business-decision making in a simulated but realistic environment.

An extensive suite of operational and financial reports for each team is produced after each round of decision making. This information is then used by the students for analysis and interpretation as well as for preparation and presentation of reports to assessors (industry executives). This is the *enrichment factor* developed at UBSS, where the BSG is integrated into both the Capstone (undergraduate) and Strategic Business Simulation (MBA) subjects.

UNANSWERED FUTURE EVOLUTION

COVID-19 has accelerated the dynamics of change in the WIL environment. It can be argued that the changes since March 2020 represent only incremental innovative evolutionary steps, but this begs a number of questions about the possible future radical revolution in the WIL arena. These questions include:

How are the changes to the actual work environment post-Covid to be incorporated in the WIL programs?

Some of these areas of evolutionary change relate not only to the changes in the WIL space, but also to the nature of the real business environment. Are changes to the way people interact in the new, on-line business world now the new norm? If so, how can these be incorporated into the WIL arena?

> **Can the move to the new virtual world in business lead to the development and use of superior forms of experiential learning in the workplace?**

CONCLUSION

While the future development of work-integrated learning platforms is unknown, what is clear is that COVID-19 has provided the catalyst to accelerate adaptation and evolution.

It remains to be seen what these developments will provide in terms of student experiential learning and the degree of involvement and interaction with academic and work skill enrichment.

The appropriate response to the COVID-induced increase in online learning is not to change the nature of WIL but to adapt the WIL delivery platform to optimise *experiential enrichment* for the student and enhance the employer's workplace.

It is also clear that there is the potential for a new industry outside the higher education arena to seize the opportunity of gamification of the executive learning delivery platform, potentially embedding higher education learning in the workplace itself rather than in the traditional classroom.

REFERENCES

Darwin, C. (1859). On the Origin of Species. Amazon.

Moore, J. F. (1993). Predators and Prey: A New Ecology for Competition. Harvard Business Review.

Chapter

19

The Move to Online Learning During COVID-19: Change, Acceptance, and a Stronger You

Natasha Jacques, Universal Business School Sydney

ABSTRACT

COVID-19 posed numerous challenges for governments, organizations, employees, students, and families. It also brought about enormous transformation to the teaching world, which posed challenges of its own. This article explores how the teaching staff at UBSS transitioned through this change, with an emphasis on people's minds and their ability to accept the change and come out stronger at the other end.

INTRODUCTION

COVID-19 has transformed our lifestyles, routines, and way of life into something that we had never experienced before. Looking back at the beginning of 2019, no one would have ever imagined that over the next 12 months we would be looking at the world through a different lens.

Even though we believe in the idea that change is inevitable, when it is imposed on us, we do not always accept it willingly. Whenever there is change, people instantaneously react with some degree of distress because they feel as if they have been pushed into the 'deep end' where they must navigate and combat the situation on their own. Even though many people may be going through similar circumstances, the discomfort associated with the change makes one feel isolated and alone. Moreover, the readiness to change is often met at varying levels by different individuals. Some people respond to the change promptly while others resist it.

Trimester 1 2020, Week 9, is when change at UBSS became inevitable. COVID-19 brought about many challenges and difficulties to the teaching world. The management, staff, administrators, and students at the School were all hit by a wave of unexpected situations, to which we had to respond instantly. Teaching transitioned from face-to-face to online, ushering in a period of anxiousness and mixed emotions.

I began to relate to the Bridges Transition Model (2017), which focuses on the transition to change and people's experiences of how they let go of the old and accept the new. Bridges defined 'transition' as the psychological process that people experience while they try to come to terms with the crisis caused by the change process. The initial step in coping with this transition is dealing with the endings that people have when they leave the old situation behind. Moreover, this model helps organizations and individuals effectively manage and navigate the personal and human side of change.

The Bridges model refers to the three stages of an individual experiencing change as Ending, Losing and Letting Go; The Neutral Zone; and The New Beginning.

THE FIRST STAGE: ENDING, LOSING AND LETTING GO

The first stage begins with the culmination of what was in existence. People learn to identify what they have lost and how to manage these losses. This is the phase where emotions are high, and people experience intense stress and anxiety. I recall administrative staff, lecturers and students all being in a state of shock and distress due to the fear of the unknown. People started analysing what they had lost. Students started questioning whether their course would continue. Lecturers were wondering if the number of classes they taught would be reduced.

The UBSS Management Team managed this stage effectively by being empathetic towards the emotions of both staff and students. The channels of communication were kept open, and everyone was informed of the extent and impact of the change from an Organization and Government perspective. The purpose and benefits of the change were outlined clearly, creating an atmosphere of positivity during this anxious phase. Daily emails, regular updates and broadcasts were sent to lecturers and students. Clear training guidance and adequate resources that would assist everyone in working effectively in the new online environment were provided. Had communication lines not been kept open there would have been a negative reaction to the change, which would have been a stumbling block in advancing to the next stage.

THE SECOND STAGE – THE NEUTRAL ZONE

During the second stage of the Bridges model, people are usually confused, unsure and impatient. There is some amount of resentment and scepticism towards the change activity. This stage acts as a pathway between what is left behind and what is yet to come. Numerous psychological shifts and repatterning occur at this point, which is the essence of the transition process.

It was at this juncture that the administrative staff and lecturers at UBSS began to have a heightened sense of control over their emotions and were able to contemplate on what the future of online teaching would look like. It was at this stage that reality started to take effect. The School supported this by delivering training sessions for lecturers to get up to speed with the new online technology – Microsoft Teams & Blackboard Collaborate, which had been chosen as the main modes of delivery.

Expectations were laid down and clarified at the onset so that administration staff and lecturers knew what was required to ensure that the quality of teaching was not impacted. Students were sent detailed guides on how to access their lectures using the new online platforms. Instruction guides and technical troubleshooting tips were made available to administrative staff and lecturers. Additionally, during live online classes, adequate support was offered by colleagues who acted as buddies during the initial phase of the online teaching transition. Furthermore, the IT Manager and Program Directors constantly provided remote monitoring, assistance, and feedback to the lecturers where required.

These strategies helped avoid confusion and frustration and provided a seamless transition during this stage. Some people adapted quicky while others who took longer to move forward. This stage also bred creativity and innovation. We learnt where we went wrong and how we could improve.

THE THIRD STAGE – THE NEW BEGINNING

In the third stage of the Bridges model, people are filled with a renewed sense of energy and zeal, which can impact productivity in a positive manner. People learn the new skills required to work successfully in the changed environment. Employees at UBSS began to embrace and contribute to the change. There was a sense of comfort using the online technology. There was also a greater sense of commitment to the overall goal. Management began to highlight the success of the changes to demonstrate the tangible results of the employees' hard work. Staff were appreciated and commended for their industry and dedication in adapting to the new norm. As a result, employees started to feel reoriented and renewed.

CONCLUSION

The lessons learnt through all three stages were shared and reflected on to sustain the change in the Organisation. Personally, I felt that the approach was very beneficial and provided feasible pathways to successful transition to change. Because change can be distressing, leaders and management need to understand the emotional aspects of transition and to support employees going through it. UBSS successfully achieved this.

REFERENCES

https://www.impactgrouphr.com/insights/change-management-best-practices-during-covid

https://www.lucidchart.com/blog/7-fundamental-change-management-models

https://www.mindtools.com/pages/article/bridges-transition-model.htm

https://www.sellingpower.com/2010/02/02/3745/the-seven-dynamics-of-change

https://wmbridges.com/about/what-is-transition/

http://changemanagementinsight.com/bridges-transition-model/

Compilation of References

Reference	Ch
Al-Abdullatif, A. M., Alsubaie, M. A., & Aldoughan, E. A. (2020). Exploring the Effects of Excessive Texting Through Mobile Applications on Students' Technostress and Academic Writing Skills in the Arabic Language. IEEE Access, 8, 166940-166950. doi:10.1109/access.2020.3024021	14
Al-Bashir, M., Kabir, R., and Rahman, I. (2016). The value and effectiveness of feedback in improving students' learning and professionalizing teaching in higher education. Journal of Education and Practice, 7(16), 38-41.	4
Albrahim, F. A. (2020). Online Teaching Skills and Competencies. The Turkish Online Journal of Educational Technology, 19(1), 9-20.	14
Allen, D. W. (April 2021). Covid Lockdown . A Critical Assessment of the Literature, 2.	11
Anderson, J. (2020). The Coronavirus Pandemic is Reshaping Education. Quartz Daily Brief. Retrieved from *https://qz.com/1826369/how-coronavirus-is-changing-education/*	4
Anonymous. (2020, June 3). My University's Betrayal of Truth. Quadrant.	11
Asoodar, M., Vaezi, S., and Izanloo, B. (2016). Framework to improve e-learner satisfaction and further strengthen e-learning implementation. Computers in Human Behavior, 63, 704-716.	4
Australian Council for Educational Research (ACER). (2020). Ministerial Briefing Paper on Evidence of the Likely Impact on Educational Outcomes of Vulnerable Children Learning at Home during COVID-19. Paper prepared for the Australian Government Department of Education, Skills and Employment.	4

Reference	Ch
Baran, E., & Correia, A.-P. (2014). A professional development framework for online teaching. TechTrends, 58(5), 95-101. doi:10.1007/s11528-014-0791-0	15
Bates, A. W., and Sangra, A. (2011). Managing Technology in Higher Education: Strategies for transforming teaching and learning. San Francisco, CA: Jossey-Bass Higher and Adult Education Series.	4
Bawa, P. (2016, March). Retention in Online Courses. SAGE Publishing, p. 1.	11
Betts, M. (2021). The student voice has spoken: and our response is... *https://www.campusreview.com.au/2021/03/the-student-voice-has-spoken-and-our-response-is-opinion/*	16
Blakey, C & Major, C 2019, 'Student Perceptions of Engagement in Online Course: An Exploratory Study', Online Journal of Distance Learning Administration, vol. XXII, no. 4., viewed 20 March 2021, *https://www.westga.edu/~distance/ojdla/winter224/blakeymajor224.html*	3
Bondanini, G., Giorgi, G., Ariza-Montes, A., Vega-Munoz, A., & Andreucci-Annunziata, P. (2020). Technostress Dark Side of Technology in the Workplace: A Scientometric Analysis. Int J Environ Res Public Health, 17(21). doi:10.3390/ijerph17218013	15
Bower, J. L., & Christensen, C. M. (1995). Disruptive Technologies: Catching the	8
Bradley C, Hirt, M, Hudson S, Northcote N, Smit S (2020) The Great Acceleration *https://www.mckinsey.com/business-functions/strategy-and-corporate-finance/our-insights/the-great-acceleration. Viewed 2nd April 2021.*	2
Bretag, T. & Mahmud, S. (2016). (n.d.). A conceptual framework for implementing exemplary academic integrity policy in Australian higher education, Chapter 32 in Handbook of Academic Integrity (Ed. Tracey Bretag), Springer.	12

Reference	Ch
Bretag, T. Curtis, G. Slade, C. McNeill, M. (2020) https://www.teqsa.gov.au/academic-integrity-toolkit.	12
Brod, C. (1984). Technostress: The Human Cost of the Computer Revolu tion. Addison-Wesley, Readin.	14
Brod, C. (1984). Technostress: The Human Cost of the Computer Revolu tion. Addison-Wesley, Readin.	15
Caponetto, I., Earp, J., & Ott, M. (2014). Gamification and education: A literature review. Proceedings of the European Conference on Games Based Learning, 1(1), 50-60.	14
Casanova, D., and Price, L. (2018). Moving towards sustainable policy and practice–a five level framework for online learning sustainability. Canadian Journal of Learning and Technology, 44(3).	4
CEDA (2015). Australia's Future Workforce. *https://www.ceda.com.au/ResearchAndPolicies/Research/Workfo rce-Skills/Australia-s-future-workforce.* Viewed 30th March 2021.	2
Cheawjindakarn, B., Suwannatthacote, P., and Theeraroungchaisri, A. (2012). Critical success factors for online distance learning in higher education: A review of the literature. Creative Education, 8(3), 61-66.	4
Clark, B. (2011). Moving the technology into the AU/LBS Classroom Project: Blended delivery: A literature review. Ontario: Ministry of Training, Colleges and Universities. Retrieved from *http://www.hpedsb.on.ca/ec/elearning/documents/BeaClarkes-Blendedlearningreview.pdf*	4
Clinton, J. (2020). Supporting Vulnerable Children in the Face of a Pandemic. Paper prepared for the Australian Government Department of Education, Skills and Employment. Melbourne, Australia: Centre for Program Evaluation, Melbourne Graduate School of Education, The University of Melbourne.	4

Reference	Ch
COVID-19 and Beyond for International Students. (n.d.). Retrieved from Study Australia: *https://www.studyinaustralia.gov.au/English/student-support*	11
Cressey, R. (1952). Application and verification of the differential association theory. The Journal of Criminal Law, Criminology, and Police Science . PP, 43 – 52.	12
Currey, E. (2020). Australian Universities should think twice before installing spyware on students' computers. The Strategist. Retrieved from *https://www.aspistrategist.org.au/australian-universities-should-think-twice-before-installing-spyware-on-students-computers/*	13
Darwin, C. (1859). On the Origin of Species. Amazon.	18
Davis N (2016). What is the Fourth Industrial Revolution? *https://www.weforum.org/agenda/2016/01/what-is-the-fourth-industrial-revolution/*. Viewed 29th March 2021.	2
Dawson, P. (2020). Strategies for using online invigilated exams. Retrieved from: *https://www.teqsa.gov.au/sites/default/files/strategies-for-using-online-invigilated-exams.pdf?v=16037580322*	13
Deloittes (2018). No-collar workforce: Humans and machines in one loop— collaborating in roles and new talent models. *https://www2.deloitte.com/us/en/insights/focus/tech-trends/2018/no-collar-workforce.html*. Viewed 31st March 2021.	2
Dhawan, S. (2019). Online Learning: A Panacea in the Time of COVID-10 Crisis. Journal of Educational Technology systems. Volume 49, Issue 1.	5
Dimeo, J. (2017). Online exam proctoring catches cheaters, raises concerns. Inside Higher Ed. Retrieved from *https://www.insidehighered.com/digital-learning/article/2017/05/10/online-exam-proctoring-catches-cheaters-raises-concerns*	13

Reference	Ch
Dumesnil, D. (2018). The effects of spaced repetition in online education. PhD dissertatio, Department of Electrical Engineering and Computer Science, Massachusetts Institute of Technology,.	15
Duran, D. (2016). Learning-by-teaching. Evidence and implications as a pedagogical mechanism. Innovations in Education and Teaching International, 54(5), 476-484. doi:10.1080/14703297.2016.1156011	14
Ebbinghaus, H. (2013). Memory: A contribution to experimental psychology. Annals of neurosciences, 20(4), 155-156.	15
GCA Chair and CEO Alan Manly Appointed to MACSM. (2021, April). Retrieved from Universal Business School Sydney: *https://www.ubss.edu.au/articles/2021/april/gca-chair-and-ceo-alan-manly-appointed-to-macsm/*	11
Global Corruption Index. (2020). Retrieved from Transparency International Australia: *https://transparency.org.au/global-ranking/*	11
Gonzalez T, de la Rubia MA, Hincz KP, Comas-Lopez M, Subirats L, Fort S, et al. (2020) Influence of COVID-19 confinement on students' performance in higher education. PLoS ONE 15(10).	4
González, C. (2010). What do university teachers think eLearning is good for in their teaching? Studies in Higher Education, 35, 61–78.	4
Greenhow, C. 2018, posted 2020, *https://www.sciline.org/covid-expert-quotes/online-learning#q1*	9
How to engage us. (2021, April 22). Retrieved from Department of Home Affairs: *https://www.homeaffairs.gov.au/help-and-support/how-to-engage-us/committees-and-fora/ministerial-advisory-council-on-skilled-migration*	11
http://changemanagementinsight.com/bridges-transition-model/	19

Reference	Ch
https://deborahalupton.medium.com/timeline-of-covid-19-in-australia-1f7df6ca5f23 accessed 30 March 2020.	7
https://wmbridges.com/about/what-is-transition/	19
https://www.europeandataportal.eu/en/impact-studies/covid-19/education-during-covid-19-moving-towards-e-learning	10
https://www.impactgrouphr.com/insights/change-management-best-practices-during-covid	19
https://www.lucidchart.com/blog/7-fundamental-change-management-models	19
https://www.mindtools.com/pages/article/bridges-transition-model.htm	19
https://www.sellingpower.com/2010/02/02/3745/the-seven-dynamics-of-change	19
https://www.theage.com.au/national/victoria/standing-desks-monitors-sell-out-as-australia-starts-working-from-home-20200316-p54aiv.html accessed 30 March 2021.	7
https://www.weforum.org/agenda/2020/04/coronavirus-education-global-covid19-online-digital-learning	10
Huang, W. H.-Y., & Soman, D. (2013). A Practitioner's Guide To Gamification Of Education. Report Series: Behavioural Economics in Action, 29(1), 1-39.	14
Hunter, F., & Bonyhady, N. (2020, January 14). Bushfires pose costly risk to Australia's booming international education market. The Sydney Morning Herald.	11
Inman, M (2020) Coronavirus impact on international student numbers will be felt longer than the GFC. ABC News Live Feed. May 20 - *https://www.abc.net.au/news/2020-05-20/coronavirus-impact-on-universities-research-worse-than-gfc/12264606*	1

Reference	Ch
International Graduate Outcomes Survey. (2018). Retrieved from Department of Education, Skills and Employment: *https://internationaleducation.gov.au/research/Pages/Data-and-Research.aspx*	11
International Student Support. (n.d.). Retrieved from Study Australia: *https://www.studyinaustralia.gov.au/English/student-support*	11
Israeli, A. (2020). Digital learning REMOTE a framework for teaching online. Harvard Business Publishing accessed on 28 February 2021 from *https://hbsp.harvard.edu/inspiring-minds/remote-a-framework-for-teaching-online*	8
It is not production quality that counts in Educational Videos-here's what students value most. 2020. The Conversation at *https://theconversation.com/its-not-production-quality-that-counts-in-educational-videos-heres-what-students-value-most-151573* accessed 30 March 2021	7
Jacobs, H, 2014, *https://elearningindustry.com/inspirational-elearning-quotes-for-elearning-professionals*	9
Jaggars, S. S. (2014). Choosing between online and face-to-face courses: Community college student voices. American Journal of Distance Education, 28(1), 27-38.	4
James, R., Krause, K.-L., and Jennings, C. (2010, October 1). The first-year experience in Australian universities: Findings from 1994–2009. Canberra: Commonwealth of Australia. Retrieved from *http://www.griffith.edu.au/__data/assets/pdf_file/0006/37491/FYEReport05.pdf*	4
Jamieson, A. (2018). Why higher education needs to adopt a customer experience. approach. *https://www.digitalpulse.pwc.com.au/why-higher-education-needs-customer-experience-approach/*	16
Johnson, S. (1998). Who Moved My Cheese? Putnam and Sons. New York: USA	8

Reference	Ch
Kahn, P., Everington, L., Kelm, K., Reid, I., and Watkins, F. (2017). Understanding student engagement in online learning environments: The role of reflexivity. Education Technology and Research Development, 65, 203-218.	4
Kebritchi, M., Lipschuetz, A., & Santiague, L. (2017). Issues and Challenges for Teaching Successful Online Courses in Higher Education. Journal of Educational Technology Systems, 46(1), 4-29. doi:10.1177/0047239516661713	14
Kebritchi, M., Lipschuetz, A., & Santiague, L. (2017). Issues and Challenges for Teaching Successful Online Courses in Higher Education. Journal of Educational Technology Systems, 46(1), 4-29. doi:10.1177/0047239516661713	15
Kim, C., and Woodland, D. (2020). Navigating the Financial Impact on COVID-19 on Higher Education. Retrieved from *https://www.kaufmanhall.com/ideas-resources/article/*	4
King, M. and McCullough, M. (2021). Student experience in the age of the customer. KPMG. *https://home.kpmg/au/en/home/insights/2021/03/student-experience-in-the-age-of-the-customer.html*	16
Koole, M. (2014). Identity and the itinerant online learner. The International Review of Research in Open and Distance learning, 15(1), 52–70.	15
Krause, K. L., and Coates, H. (2008). Students' engagement in first-year University. Assessment and Evaluation in Higher Education, 33(5), 493-505.	4
Kuiper, A., Solomonides, I., & Hardy, L. (2015). Time on task in intensive modes of delivery. Distance Education, 36(2), 231–245.	14

Reference	Ch
Lamb. S. (2020). Impact of Learning from Home on Educational Outcomes for Disadvantaged Children: Brief Assessment. Paper prepared for the Australian Government Department of Education, Skills and Employment by the Centre for International Research on Education Systems and the Mitchell Institute. Victoria University.	4
Latchem, C. (2017). Using ICTs and blended learning in transforming technical and vocational education and training. Commonwealth of Learning, 85.	11
Laurillard, D., Oliver, M., Wasson, B., and Hoppe, U. (2009). Implementing technology enhanced learning. In N. Balacheff, S. Ludvigsen, T. de Jong, A. Lazonder, S. Barnes, and L. Montandon (Eds.), Technology-enhanced learning: Principles and products (pp. 289–306). Berlin: Springer Science+Business.	4
Lewis, C. C., & Abdul-Hamid, H. (2006). Implementing Effective Online Teaching Practices: Voices of Exemplary Faculty. Innovative Higher Education, 31(2), 83-98. doi:10.1007/s10755-006-9010-z	15
Loughran, J. J. (2016). Effective Reflective Practice. Journal of Teacher Education, 53(1), 33-43. doi:10.1177/0022487102053001004	14
Manilow, B. 1983, personal statement to his touring band	9
Martin, F., Polly, D., Jokiaho, A., and May, B. (2017). Global standards for enhancing quality in online learning. The Quarterly Review of Distant Education, 18(2), 1-10.	4
Martin, F., Ritzhaupt, A., Kumar, S., & Budhrani, K. (2019). Award-winning faculty online teaching practices: Course design, assessment and evaluation, and facilitation. The Internet and Higher Education, 42, 34-43. doi:10.1016/j.iheduc.2019.04.001	14

Reference	Ch
Martin, F., Ritzhaupt, A., Kumar, S., & Budhrani, K. (2019). Award-winning faculty online teaching practices: Course design, assessment and evaluation, and facilitation. The Internet and Higher Education, 42, 34-43. doi:10.1016/j.iheduc.2019.04.001	15
Martinez, E. (2020). Pandemic Shakes Up World's Education Systems. Retrieved from *https://www.hrw.org/news/2020/03/19/pandemic-shakes-worlds-education-systems*	4
McClure, K. (2018). Catering to individual differences. Language magazine. *https://www.languagemagazine.com/2018/06/11/catering-to-individual-differences/*	6
Miller, C. (2021, February 23). Why Learning Preferences Are More Important Than Learning Styles. Retrieved from BIZ Library: *https://www.bizlibrary.com/blog/learning-methods/learning-preferences-versus-learning-styles/*	11
Molbaek, M. (2017). Inclusive teaching strategies – dimensions and agendas. International Journal of Inclusive Education, 22(10), 1048-1061. doi:10.1080/13603116.2017.1414578	15
Moore, J. F. (1993). Predators and Prey: A New Ecology for Competition. Harvard Business Review.	18
Nadin, S., & Cassell, C. (2006). The use of a research diary as a tool for reflexive practice. Qualitative Research in Accounting & Management, 3(3), 208-217. doi:10.1108/11766090610705407	14
Nadin, S., & Cassell, C. (2006). The use of a research diary as a tool for reflexive practice. Qualitative Research in Accounting & Management, 3(3), 208-217. doi:10.1108/11766090610705407	15
Najmaei, A., Sadeghinejad, Z. (2020). Reducing Students' Technostress in Online Classes: Three Technical Methods. UBSS Publications Series.	15

Reference	Ch
Nilson, L., Goodson, L. (2017). Online Teaching at its Best: Merging Instructional Design with Teaching and Learning Research. Wiley.	5
Noble, K. (2020). COVID-19 School Closures Will Increase Inequality Unless Urgent Action Closes the Digital Divide. Opinion. 3 April 2020. Victoria University. Retrieved from *http://www.mitchellinstitute.org.au/opinion/covid19-digital-divide/*	4
Northouse, P. G. (2013). Leadership: Theory and practice (6th ed.). Thousand Oaks, CA: Sage.	4
NSW State Government. (2020, March 23). Retrieved from Restrictions begin as schools move towards online learning: *https://education.nsw.gov.au/news/latest-news/restrictions-begin-as-schools-move-towards-online-learning*	11
O'Loughlin, D. (2020). Selecting teaching resources that meet student needs: A guide. *https://www.acer.org/au/discover/article/selecting-teaching-resources-that-meet-student-needs-a-guide*	6
Ohly, S., Sonnentag, S., Niessen, C., & Zapf, D. (2010). Diary Studies in Organizational Research. Journal of Personnel Psychology, 9(2), 79-93. doi:10.1027/1866-5888/a000009	15
Oliver, M., and Trigwell, K. (2005). Can 'blended learning' be redeemed? E-Learning, 2, 17–26.	4
Osatuyi, B., Osatuyi, T., & de la Rosa, R. (2018). Systematic Review of Gamification Research in IS Education: A Multi-method Approach. Communications of the Association for Information Systems, 42. doi:10.17705/1cais.04205	14
Panigrahi, R., Srivastava, P. R. and Sharma, D. (2018). Online learning: Adoption, continuance and learning outcome – A review of literature, International Journal of Information Management, 43, 1-14.	4

Reference	Ch
Park, J. H., & Choi, H. J. (2009). Factors Influencing Adult Learners' Decision to Drop Out or Persist in Online Learning. Educational Technology and Society, 12(4), 207–217.	14
Penny, A. R., & Coe, R. (2004). Effectiveness of consultation on student ratings feedback: A meta-analysis. Review of educational research, 74(2), 215-253.	15
Phillips, A 2017, conference on music production libraries: The 4M's, Los Angeles CA USA, October 2017	9
Prensky, M. (2001). On the Horizon. MCB University Press, Vol. 9 No. 5, October 2001- *https://www.marcprensky.com/writing/Prensky%20-%20Digital%20Natives,%20Digital%20Immigrants%20-%20Part1.pdf*	1
Qi, C. (2019). A double-edged sword? Exploring the impact of students' academic usage of mobile devices on technostress and academic performance. Behaviour & Information Technology, 38(12), 1337-1354.	14
Qi, C. (2019). A double-edged sword? Exploring the impact of students' academic usage of mobile devices on technostress and academic performance. Behaviour & Information Technology, 38(12), 1337-1354.	15
Qiang (2018) The Fourth Revolution, *https://en.unesco.org/courier/2018-3/fourth-revolution*. Viewed 31st March 2021.	2
Ragu-Nathan, T. S., Tarafdar, M., Ragu-Nathan, B. S., & Tu, Q. (2008). The consequences of technostress for end users in organizations: Conceptual development and empirical validation. Information systems research, 19(4), 417-433.	14
Ragu-Nathan, T. S., Tarafdar, M., Ragu-Nathan, B. S., & Tu, Q. (2008). The consequences of technostress for end users in organizations: Conceptual development and empirical validation. Information systems research, 19(4), 417-433.	15

Reference	Ch
Ramlatchan, M., & Watson, G. S. (2020). Enhancing instructor credibility and immediacy in online multimedia designs. Educational Technology Research and Development, 68(1), 511-528.	14
Rapanta, C., Botturi, L., Goodyear, P. et al. Online University Teaching During and After the Covid-19 Crisis: Refocusing Teacher Presence and Learning Activity. Postdigit Sci Educ 2, 923–945 (2020). *https://doi.org/10.1007/s42438-020-00155-y*	17
Roy, D., Tripathy, S., Kar, S. K., Sharma, N., Verma, S. K., and Kaushal, V. (2020). Study of knowledge, attitude, anxiety and perceived mental healthcare need in Indian population during COVID-19 pandemic. Asian Journal of Psychiatry, 51, 1-8.	4
Saxena, B. (2021, April 19). Learning Mode Preference. (I. Bosma, Interviewer)	11
Schwab, K (2017) The Fourth Industrial Revolution. Penguin UK, Great Britain.	2
Scull, J. Phillips, M. Sharma, U. & Garnier, K. (2020) Innovations in teacher education at the time of COVID19: an Australian perspective. Journal of Education for Teaching, 46:4, 497-506, DOI: 10.1080/02607476.2020.1802701	17
Singhal, P. (2019), Cheating found at UNSW up by 2000% as new detection methods used.	12
Smith, E. K., & Kaya, E. (2021). Online University Teaching at the time of COVID-19 (2020): An Australian Perspective, 9(2). *https://doi.org/10.22492/ije.9.2.11*	17
Spartacus, S. (2021, March 13). Sydney University choses to chase cash, not quality. The Spectator.	11
Stickler, U., Hampel, R., & Emke, M. (2020). A developmental framework for online language teaching skills. Australian Journal of Applied Linguistics, 3(1), 133-151. doi:10.29140/ajal.v3n1.271	15

Reference	Ch
Stone, C., & Springer, M. (2019). Interactivity, connectedness and 'teacher-presence': Engaging and retaining students online. Australian Journal of Adult Learning, 59(2), 146-169.	14
Sydney Morning Herald, 24th August 2019	12
Taleb, N. N. (2007). The Black Swan: the impact of the highly improbable. Penguin Books. London: UK.	7
Taleb, N. N. (2007). The Black Swan: the impact of the highly improbable. Penguin Books. London: UK.	8
Toth-Stub, S. (2020). Countries Face an Online Education Learning Curve: The coronavirus pandemic has pushed education systems: Online, testing countries' abilities to provide quality learning for all - retrieved from *https://www.usnews.com/news/best-countries/articles/2020-04-02/coronavirus-pandemic-tests-countries-abilities-to-create-effective-online-education*	4
UBSS Online. (n.d.). Retrieved from Universal Business School Sydney: *https://www.ubss.edu.au/ubss-online/*	11
UNESCO (2020). Education: From disruption to recovery. Retrieved from https://en.unesco.org/news/covid-19-learning-disruption-recovery-snapshot-unescos-work-education-2020.	4
Upadhyaya, P., & Vrinda. (2020). Impact of technostress on academic productivity of university students. Education and Information Technologies, 26(2), 1647-1664. doi:10.1007/s10639-020-10319-9	14
Upadhyaya, P., & Vrinda. (2020). Impact of technostress on academic productivity of university students. Education and Information Technologies, 26(2), 1647-1664. doi:10.1007/s10639-020-10319-9	15
Vox-Populi, T. (2020, November 4). Class Mode Delivery Preference. (I. Bosma, Interviewer)	11

Reference	Ch
Walker, R., Voce, J., Ahmed, J., Nicholls, J., Swift, E., Horrigan, S., and Vincent, P. (2014). 2014 survey of technology enhanced learning: Case studies. Oxford: Universities and Colleges Information Systems Association. Retrieved from *http://www.ucisa.ac.uk/groups/dsdg/asg/~/media/7BCB3F2F F0E141A79A66BC87DDB34A14.ashx*	4
Walker, R., Voce, J., and Ahmed, J. (2012). 2012 survey of technology enhanced learning for higher education in the UK. Oxford: Universities and Colleges Information Systems Association. Retrieved from *http://www.ucisa.ac.uk/groups/ssg/surveys.aspx*	4
Wang, X., Tan, S. C., & Li, L. (2020). Measuring university students' technostress in technology enhanced learning: Scale development and validation. Australasian Journal of Educational Technology, 36(4), 96-112.	15
Wang, X., Tan, S. C., & Li, L. (2020a). Measuring university students' technostress in technology enhanced learning: Scale development and validation. Australasian Journal of Educational Technology, 36(4), 96-112.	14
Wang, X., Tan, S. C., & Li, L. (2020b). Technostress in university students' technology-enhanced learning: An investigation from multidimensional person-environment misfit. Computers in Human Behavior, 105. doi:10.1016/j.chb.2019.106208	14
Wave. Harvard Business Review. 73(1), 43-53.	8
West, A (2021), UBSS Dean's message #117, 21 April 2021.	17
White, A. (2020), "May you live in interesting times: a reflection on academic integrity and accounting assessment during COVID19 and online learning", Accounting Research Journal, Vol. ahead-of-print No. ahead-of-print. *https://doi.org/10.1108/ARJ-09-2020-0317*	17

Reference	Ch
Whitfield, J. (2008). Lessons from the Transition to Online Learning: Information Technology. UBSS Publications Series.	6
Zimmerman, B. J., & Schunk, D. H. (1989). Self-Regulated Learning and Academic Achievement. New York: Springer.	11

About the Contributors

Angus Hooke

Is Professor and Senior Scholarship Fellow at Group Colleges Australia (GCA) and Professor of Business at the Australian Institute of Higher Education (AIH). His earlier positions include Chief Editor and Division Chief in the IMF, Chief Economist for BAE (now ABARE), Chief Economist for the NSW Treasury, Professor of Economics at Johns Hopkins University, Provost at ISG (Paris), and Director of the Entrepreneurship Department and Dean of the Business School (3,300 students) at the University of Nottingham, Ningbo, China. Angus has written and edited ten peer-reviewed books and authored numerous refereed journal articles.

Greg Whateley

Is Emeritus Professor and Deputy Vice Chancellor at Group Colleges Australia (GCA). Formerly, he was Chair of the Academic Board at the Australian Institute of Music and Dean of the College at Western Sydney University. He has maintained a keen interest in online learning and teaching since 2000 when he co-invented 'The Virtual Conservatorium' and has since found himself involved, some twenty years later, in the development of *the virtual school*. He is a prolific author in academic journals and books and in industry journals.

Alan Manly OAM

Is a writer, company director and entrepreneur, with over 30 years' experience in the technology and education industries.

Alan has been honoured in the Queen's Birthday 2021 Honours List with the *Medal of the Order of Australia (OAM) General Division*.

The honour is bestowed in appreciation of Alan's service to tertiary education. The citation also acknowledges his commitment to community service over a number of years.

https://honours.pmc.gov.au/honours/awards/2009147

He is a founding Director and Chief Executive Officer of the GCA Group of companies, which were among the first private colleges in Australia to implement distance learning via the Internet to overseas students. Alan is a Justice of the Peace, a Fellow of the Australian Institute of Company Directors, and a Fellow of the Australian Institute of Management. He is the author of two books, *When there Are Too Many Lawyers - There is No Justice*, and *The Unlikely Entrepreneur.*

Ashok Chanda

Is Provost – Virtual Campus at UBSS. He is passionate about 'Digital Transformation' in the education industry and has in-depth knowledge and experience in education and academic management and in compliance. Ashok has authored books on business strategy, organisational performance and strategic human resource management and has published numerous research papers in refereed journals.

Natasha Jacques

Is an Assistant Professor in the undergraduate program and the Administration Coordinator in the Office of the Dean at UBSS. Natasha completed her Bachelor of Arts degree in India and worked in the finance sector for nine years. She obtained her MBA (Accounting) at UBSS. Natasha is a member of the International Managers and Leaders (MIML) body, a CPA Ambassador, and an Associate member of The Research Society of Australia.

Anurag Kanwar

Is Director of Compliance and Continuous Improvement at Group Colleges Australia (GCA), Executive Secretary of the GCA Board of Directors, and a member of the UBSS Academic Integrity Committee, Audit and Risk Committee, and Workplace Health and Safety Committee. Anurag is also a practicing lawyer in NSW specialising in the areas of corporate governance and risk. She has written journal articles in the areas of international education and business law.

Arash Najmaei

Holds a PhD in strategic management and entrepreneurship from Macquarie University. He is currently working full time as a marketing consultant and teaching part time at various universities. His teaching interests include business research methods, strategic management, entrepreneurship, organizational change, and media management. Arash's research has been published in several journals and research books and presented at international conferences. He has also received three best-paper awards for his research in entrepreneurship and research methods.

Nilima Paul

Is Assistant Professor in Accounting at UBSS. She has Bachelor of Commerce (Honours) degree, a Graduate Certificate in Tertiary Education, a Master of Commerce degree, and a Doctor of Philosophy degree. Nilima is a member of the National Tax and Accounts Association, the Australian Institute of Training and Development, and the Association of Accounting Technicians. She has been teaching accounting to undergraduate and postgraduate students in a range of universities and colleges for more than 30 years and has won numerous awards for her commitment to teaching and learning.

Art Phillips

Is Adjunct Professor at UBSS and Director of the UBSS Centre for Entrepreneurship. He is a composer of film, television, and popular music and has worked in film and television for over 30 years. Currently, he teaches in the MBA program at UBSS, adjudicates in the institution's undergraduate program and sits on several of its committees including the UBSS Academic Senate. He is passionate about keeping his lectures engaging for his students and has a profound interest in digital and virtual teaching.

Jotsana Roopram

Is Associate Professor and Deputy Dean (Student Experience) at UBSS. Her main areas of expertise are examination management, developing academic systems, policy implementation in administrative processes and procedures, and school operations. Jotsana's research interests include governance and quality assurance in higher education, leadership, new managerialism, and online assessment.

Zahra Sadeghinejad

Graduated with a PhD in management from Macquarie University. She is an active researcher and an award-winning lecturer. Her areas of teaching expertise include marketing, media management, entrepreneurship, and quantitative methods. Dr Sadeghi's research has been published as book chapters and journal articles and has been presented at prestigious international conferences for which she has received multiple best-paper awards. Dr Sadeghi is currently a lecturer at the Universal Business School Sydney (UBSS), Central Queensland University (CQU), and the International College of Management Sydney (ICMS).

Wayne Smithson

Is Associate Professor, Program Director for the Bachelor of Accounting degree, and Chair of the Academic Integrity Committee at UBSS. He is also Finance Director for a performing arts organisation. Formerly, Wayne was Regional Finance Director of the Asia-Pacific region for a Swiss-based professional services organisation as well as owner and manager of a successful tax and accounting practice. Wayne is also a qualified CPA, a graduate member of the Australian Institute of Company Directors and a Fellow of the Institute of Managers and Leaders.

Syed Uddin

Is Assistant Professor at UBSS where he lectures in Business Management, Human Resource Management and Organisational Behaviour at UBSS. Formerly, he was a Research Fellow at the Loughborough University Business School in the United Kingdom. He has written many refereed articles that have been published in prestigious academic journals. Syed is a six-time winner of the UBSS Executive Dean's award for 'Outstanding Commitment to

Teaching and Learning' and is a recipient of the Vice Chancellor's Citation Award for outstanding contributions to student learning.

Andrew West

Is Dean of the Universal Business School Sydney (UBSS) and Provost of the Blended Campus. Formerly, he was Director of the Centre for Entrepreneurship at UBSS. Andrew has worked in academia for 14 years, following a successful 10-year career an entrepreneur and business owner/manager. His research output includes 12 peer-reviewed journal articles and numerous conference papers. Andrew continues to carry out research in the areas of marketing (especially of sophisticated technologies) and higher education (including workplace integrated learning).

Jason Whitfield

Is IT Manager at Group Colleges Australia, (GCA). He managed the introduction of Interactive Whiteboard technology, the adoption of the Moodle Learning Management System and the transition to the Amazon Web Services (AWS) cloud platform. He also facilitated the move to fully online learning by deploying ultra-modern classroom AV equipment and the Blackboard Collaborate online learning platform. Jason has a Bachelor of Technology (Information and Communication Systems) from Macquarie University, and is a member of the Australian Computer Society (ACS).

Richard Xi

Is a Senior Postgraduate Coordinator and an Assistant Professor at UBSS. His Australian education experience includes a Diploma of Business (SIT), a Diploma of Interpretation (NSIT), a Graduate Certificate in China Studies (USYD), a Graduate Certificate in Business Administration (UBSS), and a Master of Arts in Asian Studies (UNSW). He has been a keynote speaker in WSU's cross-cultural seminar program and a cultural adviser for two published books.

Notes pages

www.ingramcontent.com/pod-product-compliance
Lightning Source LLC
Chambersburg PA
CBHW070441100426

42812CB00004B/1182